The London Museums Guide

A guide to over 200 museums

When a man is tired of London, he is tired of life.
Dr Samuel Johnson (1709–84)

The same thing could be said of London's Museums.
The London Museums Guide is your key to the enormous variety on offer – from historic houses to dolls' houses, from ancient Egyptian hieroglyphs to modern communications technology. There are over 200 museums in the capital: some are famous world-wide, other smaller and more unusual collections await your personal discovery. With this book to guide you, all are within easy reach.

GRANTA EDITIONS

London Transport Services
For up-to-date information on buses, tubes and trains, telephone the London Transport Information Line on 0171-222 1234.

Published jointly by the South Eastern Museums Service, Ferroners House, Barbican, London EC2Y 8AA and Granta Editions.

Granta Editions is a wholly owned imprint of Book Production Consultants PLC.

© South Eastern Museums Service 1995 (6th edition)

ISBN 1 85757 027 8

South Eastern Museums Service
Ferroners House
Barbican
London EC2Y 8AA

Editors
Jemima Johnstone, Fiona Talbott

Cover and book design by Jim Reader, Book Production Consultants PLC, 25–27 High Street, Chesterton, Cambridge CB4 1ND.

Printed and bound by Grillford Printers Ltd, Milton Keynes

Front Cover (top left to bottom right): BT Museum, Imperial War Museum, HMS Belfast, Wimbledon Lawn Tennis Museum, Science Museum, Tate Gallery, London Transport Museum, Wimbledon Windmill Museum, Horniman Museum, Bethnal Green Museum of Childhood, Royal Armouries, Wellcome Trust Exhibitions, British Museum

The London Regional office of South Eastern Museums Service exists to improve the quality and effectiveness of local and regional museum and gallery provision throughout Greater London.

FUNDED BY

LONDON BOROUGHS GRANTS COMMITTEE

south eastern
museums service

CONTENTS

MUSEUMS IN LONDON   4

Entries are based on information provided by the Museums themselves and are correct at the time of going to press. If you have special needs or intend visiting one of the smaller museums we recommend confirming opening hours and facilities with the museum itself to ensure a successful visit.

NEW PROJECTS IN LONDON   64

Museum projects in the process of development. Some are already open to visitors by appointment.

MUSEUMS BY BOROUGH   67

Useful listing of all the museums and projects in each borough.

MUSEUMS BY SUBJECT   71

A guide to the larger or more significant collections in each category.

USEFUL ADDRESSES   77

Exhibitions and heritage venues, libraries and archives, professional and museum related bodies.

Wimbledon Lawn Tennis Museum

THE SYMBOLS

£   Admission charges (based on one full paying adult) Free
\+   £2 or less
\++   £2 – £4
\+++ Greater than £4 Concessions
V   Vending machine
☕   Light refreshments available
✗   More substantial snacks or meals
P   Parking available
⊖   Tube station
⚓   River launch
🚈   Docklands Light Railway
⇌   British Rail Station
🚌   Bus route numbers

Disabled Access Codes

Provided by ARTSLINE
☎ 0171-388 2227, the free telephone information service on the arts in Greater London for people with disabilities. Telephone ARTSLINE or the museum itself to check on specific access conditions.

W   Museum with unstepped access via main or sidedoor, wheelchair spaces and adapted toilet

X   Museum with flat or one-stepped access to exhibition area

A   Museum with 2-5 steps to exhibition area

S   Museum with many unavoidable steps and/or other obstacles for wheelchair users

G   Provision made for guide dogs

E   Hearing loop system installed. Check with museum whether in operation

(NOT SURE HOW MANY VISIT)
AUDIO TOUR (£2.50)
PERSONAL TOUR (around £3 per head
+ DONATION   for 1½ hr tour)

ALEXANDER FLEMING LABORATORY

St Mary's Hospital
Praed Street
Paddington
London W2 1NY
☎ 0171-725 6528

The tiny laboratory where Alexander Fleming made his historic discovery of penicillin has been restored to its original 1928 condition and opened to the public. There are also documentary and pictorial displays for visitors and a short video highlighting the importance of Fleming's discovery.

10.00–13.00 Mon–Thurs or by appointment.
£+ Concessions
⊖ Paddington
⇌ Paddington
🚌 7, 15, 23, 27, 36

Name of Governing Body:
St Mary's Hospital NHS Trust
Independent

ALFRED DUNHILL COLLECTION

30 Duke Street
St James's
London SW1Y 6DL
☎ 0171-495 2023 (curator)

This collection of antique pipes of all nations can be seen in the Duke Street shop during opening hours (09.30–17.30 Mon–Fri, 09.30–17.00 Sat). At 60/61 Burlington Arcade a collection of antique Dunhill motoring accessories, lighters, watches and pens can be viewed by appointment.

£ Free   X   G
⊖ Green Park, Piccadilly
🚌 9, 14, 19, 22, 38

Name of Governing Body:
Alfred Dunhill Limited
Independent

ALL HALLOWS BY THE TOWER UNDERCROFT MUSEUM 🌐

Byward Street
London EC3R 5BJ
☎ 0171-481 2928

One of the city's oldest churches, All Hallows contains a collection illustrating its history and that of some of the people who have been connected with it, including William Penn, the founder of Pennsylvania, who was baptised here. The Mariner's Chapel contains models of ships, given to the church in thanksgiving.

10.00–16.30. Large parties by appointment only.
£++ (audio guide)   W   S
⊖ Tower Hill
🚇 Tower Gateway
⇌ Fenchurch St
🚌 15, 25, 42, 78, 100, D1, D9, D1, X15

Name of Governing Body:
All Hallows Church
Independent

AMALGAMATED ENGINEERING AND ELECTRICAL UNION COLLECTION

110 Peckham Road
London SE15 5EL
☎ 0171-703 4231

This one-room museum tells the history of the union from its origins at the beginning of the 19th century. The displays include examples of engineering products made by members.

09.00–17.00 Mon–Fri by appointment.
£ Free   S   G   Ⓥ
⊖ Oval
⇌ Peckham Rye
🚌 12, 36, 171, 702X

Name of Governing Body:
Amalgamated Engineering and Electrical Union
Independent   £4.50
60,000 🎟 £3.00/con

APSLEY HOUSE, THE WELLINGTON MUSEUM 🌐

149 Piccadilly
Hyde Park Corner
London W1V 9FA
☎ 0171-499 5676

The Iron Duke's London palace houses his famous collection of paintings, porcelain, silver, orders, decorations and personalia. It will be re-opening in summer 1995 after major refurbishment.

11.00–17.00 Tues–Sunday.
£++ Concessions   S   G
⊖ Hyde Park Corner
⇌ Victoria
🚌 2, 8, 9, 10, 14, 16, 19, 22, 36, 38, 52, 73, 74, 82, 137, 137A

Name of Governing Body:
Trustees of the Victoria & Albert Museum
National

ARSENAL FOOTBALL CLUB MUSEUM

Arsenal Stadium
Highbury
London N5 1BU
☎ 0171-359 0808

The museum tells the 109-year history of the club, from the day in 1886 when munition workers in the Royal Oak pub first decided to form a football team. You can also find out about some of the great players and see items of memorabilia, including Alex James' shirt from the 1936 FA Cup Final.

9.30–16.00 Fri & some Public Hols (telephone for details).
£+ Concessions   X   ◨
⊖ Arsenal
⇌ Finsbury Park
🚌 4, 19, 236

Name of Governing Body:
Arsenal Football Club
Independent

ARTS COUNCIL COLLECTION

Exhibitions Department
South Bank Centre
Royal Festival Hall
London SE1 8XX
☎ 0171-921 0875

Largest collection of post-war contemporary art in the UK. The collection has no permanent exhibition space, many of the works being on long-term loan to other museums and galleries throughout Britain, but temporary exhibitions are held at the Royal Festival Hall and occasionally at the Hayward Gallery and are toured around the UK.

Limited access by appointment.
£ Free (Hayward Gallery charges admission) 🗭 X ◨
⊖ Embankment, Waterloo
⇌ Waterloo

Arsenal Football Club Museum

🚌 1, 4, 26, 68, 76, 77, 149, 168, 171, 171A, 176, 188, 501, 505, 521, D1, D11, P11, X68

Name of Governing Body:
The Arts Council of England
National Chingford
now in *doesn't know*

BADEN-POWELL HOUSE ●

65 Queen's Gate
London SW7 5JS
☎ 0171-584 7030

The headquarters of the Scout Association houses the Baden-Powell story, a permanent exhibition in words, sound and pictures on the life of the founder of the Boy Scout movement. The collection includes his dress uniform and medals, as well as mementos of some of the campaigns he fought in.

09.00–18.00 Daily.
£ Free   W   G
⊖ South Kensington, Gloucester Rd
🚌 9, 9A, 10, 14, 52, 70, 74, C1

Name of Governing Body:
The Scout Association
Independent

Baden-Powell House

BANK OF ENGLAND MUSEUM

(entrance in Bartholomew Lane)
Threadneedle Street
London EC2R 8AH
☎ 0171-601 5545 (recorded information)

A fascinating insight into the history of one of the world's most famous banks, from its founding in 1694 to the present day. Displays include a magnificent reconstruction of Sir John Soane's 1793 Stock Office, a unique collection of banknotes and gold bars and an interactive video

5

[handwritten annotations: "Some free exhibs, some pay exhibs £7 — conc/£5 3 shows per year: 22,000 per show (approx 120k part)"]

display which allows you to investigate the high-tech world of modern banking.

10.00–17.00 Mon–Fri. Closed weekends, Public & Bank Hols. Open on the day of the Lord Mayor's Show.
£ Free A G
🚇 Bank, Monument
🚄 Liverpool St, Fenchurch St, Cannon St
🚌 8, 11, 15B, 21, 22B, 23, 25, 26, 43, 76, 133, 149, 501, D9, X15, X43

Name of Governing Body:
Governor and Company of the Bank of England
Independent

[handwritten: "lots exhibs free OR £2.50 20,000 per £2/kun"]

BANKSIDE GALLERY

48 Hopton Street
London SE1 9JH
☎ 0171-928 7521

The gallery holds changing exhibitions of contemporary work by the Royal Watercolour Society and the Royal Society of Painter–Printmakers, as well as occasional historical exhibitions and educational programmes. The Diploma collections of the two societies are on long-term loan to other museums.

During exhibitions only –
10.00–20.00 Tues, 10.00–17.00 Wed–Fri, 13.00–17.00 Sun. Closed Mon & Sat.
£ ++ Concessions X Ⓥ
🚇 Blackfriars, London Bridge, Waterloo
🚄 London Bridge, Waterloo
🚌 45, 63, 149, 172, D1, D11, P11

Name of Governing Body:
The Royal Watercolour Society and the Royal Society of Painter–Printmakers
Independent

BARBICAN ART GALLERY

Gallery Floor
Barbican Centre
London EC2Y 8DS
☎ 0171-638 4141 ext 7619

The gallery, part of the Barbican Arts Centre, stages an exciting programme of major exhibitions. It has developed an international reputation for displays of 19th- and 20th-century art and photography.

10.00–18.45 Mon & Wed–Sat, 10.00–17.45 Tues, 12.00–18.45 Sun.
£+++ Concessions W E G
📷 ✗ Ⓟ
🚇 Moorgate, Barbican, St Paul's, Liverpool St
🚄 Moorgate, Liverpool St
🚌 4, 8, 11, 22B, 25, 76, 141, 172, 214, 271, 521

Name of Governing Body:
Corporation of London
Local Authority

BARNET MUSEUM

31 Wood Street
Barnet
Herts. EN5 4BE
☎ 0181-440 8066

The museum tells the history of the local area, from the Battle of Barnet in 1471 to the present day. Included in its wonderful collection of women's clothing are 19th-century wedding dresses worn by brides at Barnet churches.

14.30–16.30 Tues–Thurs, 10.00–12.00 & 14.30–16.30 Sat.
£ Free W
🚇 High Barnet
🚄 New Barnet
🚌 34, 84, 84A, 107, 234, 263, 307, 326, 384, 385, 399

Name of Governing Body:
Barnet and District Local History Society
Independent

BEN URI ART SOCIETY

4th Floor
21 Dean Street
London W1V 6NE
☎ 0171-437 2852

The society mounts regular exhibitions of contemporary Jewish art as well as of works from its permanent collection of

Ben Uri Art Society

6

paintings, prints, drawings and sculptures by Jewish artists including Bomberg, Gertler and Auerbach. A full programme of activities is provided for members of the society, including lectures, concerts and visits.

10.00–17.00 Mon–Thurs, 14.00–17.00 Sun during exhibitions.
Closed Jewish festivals and Public Hols.
£ Free   X
⊖ Oxford Circus, Tottenham Court Rd, Leicester Sq
🚌 7, 8, 10, 25, 55, 73, 98, 176

Name of Governing Body:
Ben Uri Art Society
Independent

BETHLEM ROYAL HOSPITAL ARCHIVES AND MUSEUM

The Bethlem Royal Hospital
Monks Orchard Road
Beckenham
Kent BR3 3BX
☎ 0181-776 4307/4227

The Bethlem Royal Hospital (the original 'Bedlam', founded in 1247) houses a collection of works by talented artists suffering from mental disorder. These include Richard Dadd, Louis Wain, Vaslav Nijinsky, Jonathan Martin and Charles Sims. Selected paintings and drawings from the collection are on display in the museum.

09.30–17.30 Mon–Fri. Please telephone to confirm before visiting.
£ Free   X G ▣
⇌ Eden Park, East Croydon
🚌 119, 166, 194, 198

Name of Governing Body:
The Bethlem Art and History Collections Trust
Independent

About 1,000. but it varies from year to year free

BETHNAL GREEN MUSEUM OF CHILDHOOD

Cambridge Heath Road
London E2 9PA
☎ 0181-980 2415 (recorded information)

The nation's collection of toys, dolls, games, puppets and children's clothes. One of the highlights is the display of dolls' houses on the ground floor, ranging from a royally furnished 17th-century mansion to a 1930s holiday villa.

10.00–17.50 Mon–Thurs & Sat, 14.30–17.50 Sun.
£ Free   S ▣ ▣
⊖ Bethnal Green
⇌ Cambridge Heath (restricted service)
🚌 8, 26, 48, 55, 106, 253, 309, D6

Name of Governing Body:
Trustees of the Victoria & Albert Museum
National Free, they will get back to us on figures

BEXLEY MUSEUM

Hall Place
Bourne Road
Bexley 70,000
Kent DA5 1PQ
☎ 01322-526574 ext 209

This intriguing Tudor house constructed from rubble masonry (probably taken from destroyed medieval monasteries) with a red-brick 17th-century extension, houses collections relating to the history of the local area and its natural environment.

10.00–17.00 Mon–Sat , 14.00–18.00 Sun (summer only). Closes dusk if earlier.
£ Free   S ▣ X ▣
⇌ Bexley
🚌 132, 857, B15

Name of Governing Body:
London Borough of Bexley
Local Authority

Bexley Museum

7

I get back tous

ᴌACK CULTURAL ARCHIVES/MUSEUM

378 Coldharbour Lane
Brixton
London SW9 8LF
☎ 0171-738 4591
(fax 0171-738 7168)

The story of Black people in Britain told through African artefacts, slave papers, records and photographs.

Museum 10.00–18.00 Mon–Sat, Archives 10.00–16.00 by appointment only.
£ Free X
⊖ Brixton
≷ Brixton
🚍 2, 3, 35, 37, 45, 45A, 109, 118, 133, 159, 196, 250, 322, 689, P4, P5

Name of Governing Body:
The African Peoples Historical Monument Foundation (UK)
Independent

BRITISH OXYGEN COMPANY MUSEUM

(The Charles King Collection)
9 Bedford Square
London WC1B 3RA
☎ 0171-631 1650

The British Oxygen Company Museum houses the Charles King Collection of historic anaesthetic apparatus.

Open for research by appointment.
£ Free A G
⊖ Tottenham Court Rd, Russell Sq
🚍 10, 14, 14A, 24, 29, 73, 134

Name of Governing Body:
The Association of Anaesthetists of Great Britain & Ireland
Independent

← WRONG NUMBER
(ASSOCIATION OF BRITISH ANETHETISTS)

BOSTON MANOR HOUSE

Boston Manor Road
Brentford
Middlesex TW8 9JX
☎ 0181-570 0622

This Jacobean manor house, built in 1623, now houses a small display on the history of the area. You can also view some of the rooms, including the State Bedroom and a drawing room with a magnificent panelled ceiling.

End May–end Sept: 14.30–17.00 Sun.
£ Free S P
⊖ Boston Manor
≷ Brentford
🚍 E8

Name of Governing Body:
London Borough of Hounslow
Local Authority

BRAMAH TEA AND COFFEE MUSEUM

Clove Building
Maguire Street
Butlers Wharf
London SE1 2NQ
☎ 0171-378 0222 *number not recogn*

The fascinating story of tea and coffee and their effect on our daily lives from the 17th century to the present day. The collection includes a wonderful selection of teapots and coffee-making machines from around the world; as well as cartoons, prints and paintings, all relating to the history of tea and coffee.

10.00–18.30 Daily. Closed 25 & 26 Dec.
£++ Concessions V 🍵
⊖ Tower Hill
🚈 Tower Gateway, London Bridge
≷ London Bridge
🚍 42, 47, 78, 188, 705, P11

Name of Governing Body:
Private collection
Independent

will call back

BRITISH COUNCIL COLLECTION

Visual Arts Department
11 Portland Place
London W1N 4EJ
☎ 0171-389 3049

Major collection of 20th-century British art including paintings, sculpture, watercolours, graphics, photographs and mixed media works, mainly intended for world-wide circulating exhibitions.

Access by written appointment only.
£ Free
⊖ Oxford Circus
🚍 3, 6, 7, 8, 10, 12, 13, 16A, 25, 53, 55, 73, 88, 94, 98, 135, 137, 139, 159, 17, 6, C2, X53

Name of Governing Body:
British Council
National

BRITISH DENTAL ASSOCIATION MUSEUM

64 Wimpole Street
London W1M 8AL
☎ 0171-935 0875 ext 209/211

Dental equipment, furniture, reconstructed surgeries and cartoon prints illustrate the history of British dentistry from the 18th century. Displays also show aspects of the dentist's work, such as denture making and tooth extraction.

10.00–15.30 Mon–Fri. Closed Bank Hols.
£ Free A
⊖ Oxford Circus, Regent's Park, Bond Street
🚍 3, 6, 7, 8, 10, 12, 13, 15, 16A,

23, 25, 55, 73, 88, 94, 98, 113, 135, 137, 139, 159, 176, C2

Name of Governing Body:
British Dental Association
Independent
~~contact~~ ~~els standard~~
0207 323 8000

BRITISH MUSEUM ✓ ●

Great Russell Street
London WC1B 3DG
☎ 0171-636 1555

National collection of antiquities, ethnography, prints, drawings, coins, medals and banknotes. The museum departments are: Greek and Roman, Egyptian, Japanese, Prehistoric and Romano-British, Western Asiatic, Oriental, Coins and Medals, Medieval and Later, Prints and Drawings and Ethnography.

10.00–17.00 Mon–Sat;
14.30–18.00 Sun.
£ Free   W   X   G   E   ⊕   ✗
⊖ Tottenham Court Rd, Holborn, Russell Sq
🚌 7, 8, 10, 14, 19, 22B, 24, 25, 29, 30, 38, 55, 68, 73, 91, 98, 134, 168, 176, 1, 88

Name of Governing Body:
Trustees of the British Museum
National 5, 735, 399

Average special exhib

BRITISH OPTICAL
ASSOCIATION MUSEUM   Price = £7

c/o British College of Optometrists
10 Knaresborough Place
London SW5 OTG
☎ 0171-373 7765   NOT RECOGNISED

Hand-carved spectacles, a Wedgwood spyglass and a 19th-century specimen viewer are just some of the items used to illustrate optical history from the Middle Ages. The museum also contains a variety of prints, paintings, sculpture and china – all featuring spectacle-wearers.

10.00–16.00 Mon–Fri by appointment only. Not suitable for groups of more than six.
£ Free   S
⊖ Earl's Court
🚌 31, 49, 74, C1, C3

Name of Governing Body:
British College of Optometrists
Independent
will call us

BROMLEY MUSEUM   ●

The Priory
Church Hill
Orpington BR6 OHH
☎ 01689-873826

15, 500

FREE

This impressive medieval/post-medieval building houses the Avebury collection, local archaeological material from the Palaeolithic to the early Saxon periods, geological material and expanding collections of social history, dress and fine art.

09.00–17.00 Mon–Wed, Fri, Sat.
Closed Bank Hols.
£ Free   S   G   ℙ
🚋 Orpington
🚌 51, 61, 208, R1, R3, R4, R7, R11

Name of Governing Body:
London Borough of Bromley
Local Authority
Carol Part
01 380 816 565

BROOKING COLLECTION   ●

University of Greenwich
Dartford Campus
Oakfield Lane   part
Dartford   @
Kent DA1 2SZ   care4free
☎ 0181-331 9897   . net

This amazing collection of architectural pieces, gathered together by one man, numbers over 25, 000 items. It includes balustrades, bootscrapers, doors, sash-windows, skylights, pediments and pilasters ranging from 16th century to the present day and from the grand to the very ordinary.

09.00–17.00 Mon–Fri by appointment only.
£ Free   W   ℙ
🚋 Dartford
🚌 476, 478

Name of Governing Body:
Brooking Architectural Museum Trust
Independent
1200 per year

British Museum

Also Devices Museum Salisbury = 22,000 per anum

will ring back

BRUCE CASTLE MUSEUM

Lordship Lane
London N17 8NU
☎ 0181-808 8772

Built in the 16th century, but
substantially altered in later years,
Bruce Castle was once the home
of Rowland Hill, the inventor of
the Penny Post, whose family ran
a boys' school in the building.
Displays include the local history
of Haringey, a fine postal history
collection and temporary
exhibitions on a variety of themes.

13.00–17.00 Wed–Sun.
£ (Free) A G 🅿
⊖ Wood Green
⇌ Bruce Grove
🚌 123, 243, 243A

Name of Governing Body:
London Borough of Haringey
Local Authority

BRUNEL'S ENGINE HOUSE

Tunnel Road
Rotherhithe
London SE16 4LF
☎ 0181-318 2489
☎ 01233-770355

Part of the temporary works for
Marc Isambard Brunel's Thames
Tunnel, the world's first
underwater thoroughfare. The
tunnel is still in use by
London Underground's
East London Line, and
the Engine House is

Brunel's Engine House

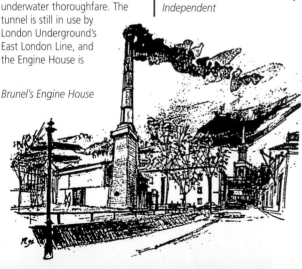

now a museum housing a
restored steam engine and a
display about the Thames Tunnel.

12.00–16.00 first Sun of each
month or otherwise by
appointment.
£ + Concessions   S
⊖ Rotherhithe
🚌 47, 188, P11

Name of Governing Body:
Brunel Exhibition Rotherhithe
Independent

BT MUSEUM

145 Queen Victoria Street
London EC4V 4AT
☎ 0171-248 7444,
☎ 0800-289689 (free information
line).

BT's prize-winning museum tells
the story of 200 years of
telecommunications history
through a series of 'touch and try'
displays, videos and exhibits from
the historical collection.

10.00–17.00 Mon–Fri.
£ ++ Concessions   S   G
⊖ Blackfriars, St Paul's
⇌ Blackfriars
🚌 45, 63, 172

Name of Governing Body:
British Telecommunications plc
Independent

CABINET WAR ROOMS

Clive Steps
King Charles Street
London SW1A 2AQ
☎ 0171-930 6961

The underground emergency
headquarters used by Winston
Churchill and the British
government during World War II.
Visitors can see the room in which
Churchill made some of his most
famous BBC broadcasts and the
Map Room, the nerve centre of
the complex, where the latest
information on the progress of
the war was collected and
analysed.

April–end Sept, 9.30–18.00 Daily.
Oct–end March, 10.00–18.00
Daily. Closed 24–26 Dec & 1 Jan.
£ ++ Concessions   W   G
⊖ Westminster
🚌 3, 11, 12, 24, 53, 77A, 88,
109, 159, 184, 196

Name of Governing Body:
Imperial War Museum
National
will phone back

CARLYLE'S HOUSE

24 Cheyne Row
Chelsea
London SW3 5HL
☎ 0171-352 7087

This 18th-century town house
was the home of the writer
Thomas Carlyle (1795–1881) and
his wife Jane. It contains their
books, personalia and furniture,
including an early piano played by
Chopin.

Apr–Oct, 11.00–17.00 Wed–Sun
& Bank Hol Mons. Closed Good
Friday.
£ ++   S   G
⊖ South Kensington, Sloane Sq
🚌 11, 19, 22, 45A, 49, 211, 239,
249

£3.60

Name of Governing Body:
The National Trust
Independent

CARSHALTON WATER TOWER

Carshalton House
Pound Street
Carshalton
Surrey SM5 3PS
☎ 0181-647 0984

The grounds of Carshalton manor house contain a unique survival of 18th-century domestic architecture – a water tower complete with a pump chamber, a robing room, a bathroom with a magnificent tiled plunge bath and an orangery.

Water Tower: Open first Sun in every month, Apr–Oct.
Hermitage: Open 14.00–17.00 every Sun, Apr–Oct.
Open days & groups by appointment –telephone for details
£ +
⇌ Carshalton
🚍 127, 154, 157, 407, 408, 413, 726

Name of Governing Body:
Carshalton Water Tower Trust
Independent

CAT MUSEUM

49 High St
Harrow on the Hill
Middlesex
HA1 3HT
☎ 0181-422 1892

A collection of antique cats from around the world, depicted in all media: pottery, porcelain, glass, silver, bronze, base metals, paintings, drawings, prints, needlework, leather, wood and ivory.

9.30–17.00 Thurs–Sat,
14.00–17.00 Sun

£ Free
⊖ Harrow on the Hill, South Harrow
⇌ Harrow, Wealdstone
🚍 258, H17

Name of Governing Body:
Privately owned
Independent

CHARLES DARWIN MEMORIAL MUSEUM

Down House
Luxted Road
Downe
Orpington
Kent BR6 7JT
☎ 01689-859 119

This country house is where Charles Darwin lived from 1842 until his death in 1882 and where he wrote *On The Origin of Species*. It is still furnished as it was in his time and contains many of his possessions, including the diary he kept during his voyage on the *HMS Beagle*.

13.00–18.00 Wed–Sun & Bank Hol Mons.
£ ++ Concessions X G 🅿
⇌ Bromley South
🚍 146

BT Museum

Name of Governing Body:
The Natural History Museum
Independent
7417 4430
they don't know.

CHARTERED INSURANCE INSTITUTE MUSEUM

The Hall
20 Aldermanbury
London EC2V 7HY
☎ 0171-606 3835

In the 17th century the only effective firefighting service was that provided by insurance companies to their clients. To prove that the home-owner had taken out a policy and was entitled to assistance, the company in question required their official firemark to be displayed on the outside of the house. A unique collection of these firemarks and fireplates is on display in the museum, together with other artefacts relating to the history of firefighting and fire insurance.

09.00–17.00 Mon–Fri, please telephone in advance, if possible, on 0171-417 4417

14,223

Chiswick House

£ Free S G
⊖ Moorgate, Bank, St Paul's
⇌ Moorgate
🚌 4, 8, 21, 22B, 25, 43, 76, 141, 172

Name of Governing Body:
Chartered Insurance Institute
Independent

CHELSEA PHYSIC GARDEN

(entrance on Swan Walk)
66 Royal Hospital Road
London SW3 4HS
☎ 0171-352 5646

One of Europe's oldest botanic gardens, the Chelsea Physic Garden was founded in 1673 by the Society of Apothecaries to help their study of the therapeutic properties of plants. Displays include Chinese medicinal plants and herbs, plants used in present day medicine and those currently undergoing research. In addition there are glasshouses, botannical order beds and the oldest rock garden in Europe.

Apr–end Oct: 14.00–17.00 Wed, 14.00–18.00 Sun. Chelsea Flower Show & Chelsea Festival week: 12.00–17.00.

£++ Concessions X G 🍵
⊖ Sloane Sq
🚌 11, 19, 22, 211, 239

Name of Governing Body:
Chelsea Physic Garden Company
Independent

CHISWICK HOUSE

Burlington Lane
Chiswick
London W4 2RP
☎ 0181-995 0508

The ornate reception rooms of this 18th century English Palladian villa are decorated in their original manner and adorned with some of the original pictures. The ground floor exhibition illustrates the evolution of the house and gardens.

1 Oct–31 Mar, 10.00–16.00 Wed–Sun.
1 Apr–30 Sept, 10.00–13.00 & 14.00–18.00 Daily.
Closed 24–26 Dec & 1 Jan.
£++ Concessions S G 🍵 ✗ 🅿
⊖ Turnham Green
⇌ Chiswick
🚌 190, 290, 415, E3

Name of Governing Body:
English Heritage
Nationally funded

CHURCH FARMHOUSE MUSEUM ✏

Greyhound Hill
Hendon
London NW4 4JR
☎ 0181-203 0130

This charming 17th-century farmhouse, the oldest in the parish of Hendon, now houses reproductions of a fully furnished 19th-century dining room, a scullery and a kitchen crammed with ingenious gadgets – from a salamander (for browning puddings) to sugarcutters. There are also changing exhibitions on local history, crafts and the decorative arts.

10.00–17.00 Mon–Thurs,
10.00–13.00 & 14.00–17.30 Sat,
14.00–17.30 Sun.
£ Free S G 🅿
⊖ Hendon Central
⇌ West Hendon
🚌 113, 143, 183, 326

Name of Governing Body:
London Borough of Barnet
Local Authority

call back later
not interested!

CLINK PRISON MUSEUM ✏

1 Clink Street   in us
London SE1 9DG
☎ 0171-378 1558,
☎ 0171-403 6515

The museum tells the history of the Clink Prison and the 'Liberty of the Clink' – once London's red-light district, up till 1780. The museum's collection includes torture instruments and scenes depicting life in Southwark and Bankside in the 18th century.

10.00–18.00 Daily.
£++ Concessions S
⊖ London Bridge

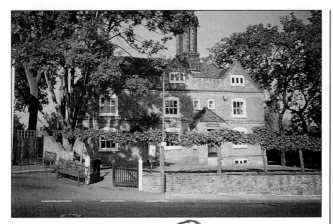

Church Farmhouse Museum

≋ London Bridge
🚌 17, 21, 22A, 35, 43, 46, 47, 48, 133, 149, 344, 505, 521, 705, D1, D11, P3, P11, X43

Name of Governing Body:
Privately owned *call back*
Independent *ten minutes*

CLOCKMAKERS' COMPANY COLLECTION *♠*

The Clock Room
Guildhall Library
Aldermanbury
London EC2P 2EJ
☎ 0171-606 3030 ext 1865

A prize of £20, 000 was offered by the British government in 1714 to the clockmaker who could solve the problem of perfect marine timekeeping; it was eventually won by John Harrison. Examples of his work are among the clocks and watches on display from the Clockmakers' Collection. You can also see Earnshaw's chronometer watch of 1791, used in the discovery of Vancouver.

09.30–16.45 Mon–Fri. Closed weekends & Bank Hols.

 £ Free X
⊖ St Paul's, Moorgate, Bank, Mansion House
≋ Liverpool St, Moorgate
🚌 4, 8, 11, 15B, 21, 22B, 25, 26, 43, 76, 133, 172, 501, X43

Name of Governing Body:
Worshipful Company of Clockmakers
Independent

COMMONWEALTH INSTITUTE

Kensington High Street
London W8 6NQ
☎ 0171-603 4535

Discover the history, culture, wildlife, crafts and economies of the 50 Commonwealth countries through a programme of permanent and special exhibitions, cultural events, festivals and the Education Programme for schools. Contact the Information Centre for a free copy of *What's On.*

10.00–17.00 Mon–Sat,
14.00–17.00 Sun.
£+ Concessions W E G ✗
⊖ High St Kensington, Earl's Court, Holland Park, Olympia
≋ Kensington Olympia
🚌 9, 9A, 10, 27, 28, 31, 49, C1

Name of Governing Body:
Board of Governors of the Commonwealth Institute
National

COURTAULD INSTITUTE GALLERIES *♠*

Somerset House
Strand
London WC2R ORN
☎ 0171-873 2526 *NOT RECOGNISED*

These galleries contain the wonderful Samuel Courtauld

Commonwealth Institute
NO RECORD KEPT

Collection of Impressionist and Post-Impressionist paintings, which includes works by Manet, Renoir, Cézanne, Van Gogh and Gauguin. The building also houses the Princes Gate Collection of Old Master paintings, the Lee and Gambier-Parry Collections and the Hunter Bequest.

10.00–18.00 Mon–Sat, 14.00–18.00 Sun. Closed 24–26 Dec.
£++ Concessions X G ☕
⊖ Temple, Covent Garden
≋ Charing Cross, Waterloo
🚌 1, 4, 6, 9, 11, 13, 15, 23, 26, 68, 77A, 168, 171, 171A, 176, 188, 501, 505, 521

Name of Governing Body:
University of London
University ᴡⁱˡˡ ᶜᵃˡˡ ᵇᵃᶜᵏ

CRAFTS COUNCIL ●

44A Pentonville Road
London N1 9BY
☎ 0171-278 7700

National centre for contemporary craft, housing a gallery with changing exhibitions, as well as an information centre, reference and picture libraries and a loan collection.

11.00–18.00 Tues–Sat, 14.00–18.00 Sun.
£ Free W G ☕
⊖ Angel
≋ King's Cross
🚌 4, 19, 30, 38, 43, 56, 73, 153, 171A, 214, X43

Name of Governing Body:
The Crafts Council
National

CROYDON CLOCKTOWER

(Lifetimes, Riesco Gallery & Clocktower Gallery)
Katharine St
Croydon CR9 1ET
☎ 0181-253 1030

This new museum, arts and library complex, opened in spring 1995, contains the following attractions. Lifetimes – a unique interactive exhibition about Croydon's people. The Riesco Gallery – a display of Chinese ceramics from 4500BC to the 19th century. The Clocktower Gallery – showing a range of unusual and interactive exhibitions.

12.00–18.00 Mon–Fri, 12.00–17.00 Sat & Sun. Closed 25 & 26 Dec.
Lifetimes: £+ Concessions
Riesco Gallery: £ Free W G ☕

Courtauld Institute Galleries

≋ East Croydon, West Croydon
🚌 50, 54, 60, 64, 68A, 75, 109, 119, 130, 154, 157, 166, 198, 250, 264, 301, 312, 403, 405, 407, 409, 498, 726

Name of Governing Body:
London Borough of Croydon
Local Authority
ɴᴏ ʟᴏɴɢᴇʀ ᴇxɪsᴛs

CROYDON NATURAL HISTORY AND SCIENTIFIC SOCIETY MUSEUM ◍

c/o 96a Brighton Road
South Croydon
Surrey CR2 6AD
☎ 0181-688 2720

Collections relating to local geology, archaeology, natural and social history.

Open by appointment.
£ Free A
≋ Woodmansterne
🚌 50, 68A, 109, 166, 312, 407

Name of Governing Body:
Croydon Natural History and Scientific Society
Independent

Croydon Clocktower

CRYSTAL PALACE MUSEUM

Anerley Hill
London SE19 2BA
☎ 0181-676 0700

The Crystal Palace was erected in Hyde Park in 1851 to house the Great Exhibition and proved so popular that when the exhibition ended it was taken down and re-erected on Sydenham Heights. It attracted thousands of visitors until 1936, when it burned down in one of the most spectacular fires ever seen. The museum, located in the only part of the building that survived, tells the fascinating story of this 'Palace of the People'.

11.00–17.00 Sun & Bank Hol Mons.
£ Free P
≈ Crystal Palace
🚌 2, 3, 63, 122, 137A, 157, 202, 227, 249, 306, 322, 358, 450

Name of Governing Body:
The Crystal Palace Museum Trust
Independent

CUMING MUSEUM

155–157 Walworth Road
London SE17 1RS
☎ 0171-701 1342

Fascinating displays of everyday objects, from Roman times to the present, illustrate the history of Southwark's people. The collection was gathered by the Cuming family (c.1790–1900) and also includes archaeology, ethnography and decorative art from around the world. The museum is a former winner of the National Heritage Museum of the Year Award.

10.00–17.00 Tues–Sat
£ Free S G P

⊖ Elephant and Castle
≈ Elephant and Castle
🚌 12, 35, 40, 45, 68, 171, 176, X68

Name of Governing Body:
London Borough of Southwark
Local Authority

CUTTY SARK THE CLIPPER SHIP

King William Walk
Greenwich
London SE10 9HT
☎ 0181-858 3445

The last surviving tea clipper was famous in her day for making the fastest voyage from China to England, completed in 107 days. She is now moored in dry dock at Greenwich and has been painstakingly restored to her condition in the 1870s. Visitors can explore the ship from the elegant officers' saloon to the confined living quarters of the crew. There is also a colourful collection of merchant ship figureheads on display.

Oct–Mar, 10.00–17.00 Mon–Sat, 12.00–17.00 Sun.
Apr–Sept, 10.00–18.00 Mon–Sat, 12.00–18.00 Sun.

Cutty Sark

£++ Concessions S G
🚏 Island Gardens and foot tunnel
≈ Greenwich
🚌 177, 180, 188, 286, 386

Name of Governing Body:
Maritime Trust
Independent
will phone back

CZECH MEMORIAL SCROLLS CENTRE

Westminster Synagogue
Kent House
Rutland Gardens
Knightsbridge
London SW7 1BX
☎ 0171-584 3741

A permanent exhibition tells the unique story of the rescue from Prague, in 1964, of 1, 564 Torah scrolls confiscated by the Nazis during World War II and their restoration and redistribution to communities throughout the world.

10.00–16.00 Tues & Thurs, other times by appointment.
£ Free
⊖ Knightsbridge

🚌 9, 10, 14, 19, 22, 52, 74, 137, C1

Name of Governing Body:
Memorial Scrolls Trust
Independent

DAVID EVANS CRAFT CENTRE OF SILK

Bourne Road
Crayford
Kent DA1 4BP
☎ 01322-559401

A fascinating insight into the history of silk and traditional silk craftsmanship from cocoon to finished product. Visitors can investigate replicas of a 19th-century dockside, complete with silk clipper; a block-maker's shed and a Victorian street of shops. They can also see craftsmen hand-printing silk and visit the silk craft shop.

Design Museum

09.30–17.00 Mon–Fri,
09.30–16.30 Sat.
£+ Concessions X G ☕ ℗
≋ Crayford
🚌 96, 132, 492, 726

Name of Governing Body:
David Evans & Co.
Independent

020 7403 6933

DESIGN MUSEUM ●

Butlers Wharf
Shad Thames
London SE1 2YD
☎ 0171-407 6261 (recorded information) NOT RECOGNISED

Regularly changing exhibitions and displays of cars, furniture, domestic appliances, cameras, graphics and other man-made objects offer an introduction to the role of design in our everyday lives from the origins of mass production to the present day.
11.30–18.00 Mon–Fri,

12.00–18.00 Sat & Sun.
£+++ Concessions W G ☕
X ℗
⊖ London Bridge, Tower Hill
🚇 Tower Gateway
≋ London Bridge
🚌 42, 47, 78, 188, 705, P11

Name of Governing Body:
The Conran Foundation
Independent

DICKENS HOUSE MUSEUM

48 Doughty Street
London WC1N 2LF
☎ 0171-405 2127

This house in Doughty Street is where Dickens lived with his family from 1837 to 1839 and where he wrote much of *Oliver Twist* and *Nicholas Nickleby*. It is now filled with a vast collection of furniture, pictures, letters and memorabilia associated with Dickens' life and work. Visitors

Dickens House Museum

can even see an icing sugar model of the author.

10.00–17.00 Mon–Sat. Closed Sun, Bank Hols and Christmas week.
£++ Concessions S G
⊖ Russell Sq
⇌ King's Cross
🚍 17, 19, 38, 45, 46, 55, 171A, 243, 505

Name of Governing Body:
Trustees of the Dickens House and Dickens House Fund
Independent

DIOCESAN TREASURY IN THE CRYPT OF ST. PAUL'S CATHEDRAL

Chapter House
St. Paul's Churchyard
London EC4M 8AD
☎ 0171-236 0752

The cathedral treasury holds ecclesiastical plate, manuscripts and regalia, including beautifully embroidered 19th-century vestments. The objects date from the Reformation to the present day and many are on loan from other parishes in London.

09.00–16.15 Mon–Sat
£++ Concessions
⊖ St Paul's
⇌ St Paul's Thameslink
🚍 4, 8, 11, 15, 17, 22B, 23, 25, 26, 76, 172, 501, 521, X15

Name of Governing Body:
Dean and Chapter of St. Paul's
Independent ~~will call back~~

DR JOHNSON'S HOUSE

17 Gough Square
London EC4A 3DE
☎ 0171-353 3745

The first definitive English dictionary was compiled in this

~~£140,000 people~~

house by Samuel Johnson, who lived here from 1749 to 1759. Exhibits now include first editions of the dictionary and objects relating to Johnson's life and work.

Oct–Apr, 11.00–17.00 Mon–Sat. May–Sept, 11.00–17.30 Mon–Sat. Closed Sun & Public Hols.
£++ Concessions S G
⊖ Chancery Lane, Temple, Blackfriars
⇌ St Paul's Thameslink, Blackfriars
🚍 4, 11, 15, 23, 26, 76, 171A, X15

Name of Governing Body:
Trustees of Dr Johnson's House
Independent

~~£4~~
~~£3 OAPS~~
~~free/cons~~

DULWICH PICTURE GALLERY

College Road
London SE21 7AD
☎ 0181-693 5254/0923

England's oldest public art gallery, purpose-built by Sir John Soane in the 19th century, houses an important collection of 17th- and 18th-century Old Master paintings, including works by Rembrandt, Rubens, Gainsborough and Poussin.

10.00–17.00 Tues–Fri, 11.00–17.00 Sat, 14.00–17.00 Sun.
£++ Concessions A G P
⇌ West Dulwich, North Dulwich
🚍 3, 12, 37, 40, 115, 176, 185, 312, 511, P4

~~8299 8711~~
~~will call back~~ **17**

handwritten: $8–10,000 per annum, £3.50 2.50/con

Fan Museum

Name of Governing Body:
Trustees of Dulwich Picture Gallery
Independent

EAST HAM NATURE RESERVE

Norman Road
East Ham
London E6 4HN
☎ 0181-470 4525

This nine-acre churchyard contains many species of birds, animals and plants.

10.00–17.00 Daily.
£ Free
⊖ East Ham then bus
⇌ North Woolwich, then bus
🚌 101, 104, 173, 262, 276, 300, D2

Name of Governing Body:
Governors of the Passmore Edwards Museum
Local Authority

EMBROIDERERS' GUILD

Apartment 41
Hampton Court Palace
East Molesey
Surrey KT8 9AU
☎ 0181-943 1229

A remarkable collection of British and foreign embroidered textiles dating from the 16th century to the present day. There are also visiting exhibitions in August and December.

10.30–16.00 Mon–Fri by appointment only.
£ Free ☕
🚢 from Richmond, Westminster & Kingston
⇌ Hampton Court
🚌 111, 216, 726, R68

Name of Governing Body:
The Embroiderers' Guild
Independent

ERITH MUSEUM

Erith Library
Walnut Tree Road
Erith,
Kent DA8 1RS
☎ 01322-336582

The history of Erith from the Stone Age to the modern industrial age is here on view. Displays include Thames barges and a model of the *Great Harry*, a spectacular warship fitted out in 1513 in Erith's naval dockyard.

14.15–17.15 Mon & Wed,
14.15–17.00 Sat.
£ Free   A   G
⇌ Erith
🚌 99, 229, 469, B12, B13

Name of Governing Body:
London Borough of Bexley
Local Authority

FAN MUSEUM

12 Crooms Hill
Greenwich
London SE10 8ER
☎ 0181-858 7879
☎ 0181-305 1441

The only museum in the world devoted to one of fashion's most beautiful and practical accessories. Fans and fan leaves are displayed with related and explanatory material in two listed Georgian townhouses.

11.00–16.30 Tues–Sat,
12.00–16.30 Sun. Free entry for OAPs and disabled people on Tues 14.00–16.30.
£++ Concessions   A
☕ Special bookings only.
⇌ Greenwich
🚶 Island Gardens
🚌 177, 180, 188, 199, 286, 386

Name of Governing Body:
The Fan Museum Trust Ltd
Independent   *handwritten: will call back*

FENTON HOUSE

Hampstead Grove
London NW3 6RT
☎ 0171-435 3471

Set in a delightful walled garden, this elegant William & Mary house contains a unique collection of early keyboard instruments – maintained in perfect playing condition for a series of chamber music recitals held each summer. The house also contains an outstanding collection of 17th-century Continental and English porcelain figurines.

Mar, 14.00–17.00 Sat & Sun,
Apr–end Oct, 11.00–17.30 Sat, Sun & Bank Hols. 14.00–17.30 Mon, Tues & Wed. Last admission half hour before closing.

£++ S G
⊖ Hampstead
🚌 46, 210, 268

Name of Governing Body:
The National Trust
Independent

phone on Monday 25th

FLORENCE NIGHTINGALE MUSEUM

2 Lambeth Palace Road
London SE1 7EW
☎ 0171-620 0374

Chronicles the history of this remarkable woman – her struggle to become a nurse against family and social pressures, her growing fame as the 'Lady with the Lamp' amidst the horrors of the Crimean War, and her reform of nursing and health care. At the centre of the museum is a life-sized reconstruction of a Crimean ward.

10.00–17.00 (last admission 16.00) Tues–Sun & Bank Hol Mons.
£++ Concessions W G 🅿
⊖ Waterloo, Westminster, Lambeth North
🚆 Waterloo
🚌 12, 53, 77, 109, 171, 171A, 211, 507, X53

Name of Governing Body:
The Florence Nightingale Museum Trust
Independent

Fenton House
No answer

FORTY HALL MUSEUM

Forty Hill
Enfield
Middlesex EN2 9HA
☎ 0181-363 8196

Built in 1629 for Sir Nicholas Raynton, the house retains much of its original interior. The exhibits include furniture, ceramics and glass and there is a temporary exhibitions programme.

10.00–17.00 Thurs–Sun
£ Free X G 💮 🅿
🚆 Enfield Chase, Enfield Town, Gordon Hill
🚌 191, 231

Name of Governing Body:
London Borough of Enfield
Local Authority

FREDERICK W. PAINE MUSEUM

Bryson House
Horace Road
Kingston-upon-Thames
Surrey KT1 2SL
☎ 0181-546 7472

Exhibition on the history of the Frederick W. Paine company of undertakers and on the activities of associated companies.

09.00–17.30 Mon–Fri, by appointment only.

£ Free 🅿
🚆 Kingston
🚌 71, 281, 406, 465, 479, 578, 727, K1, K3, K4, K8

Name of Governing Body:
SCI UK plc
Independent
£12,000 per annum

FREUD MUSEUM

20 Maresfield Gardens
London NW3 5SX
☎ 0171-435 2002/5167

The house where Freud lived and worked for the last year of his life. His working library, extraordinary collection of antiquities and the famous desk and couch were all brought here from Vienna when Freud was forced to flee in 1938. The museum offers insights into the sources and nature of Freud's achievements and those of his daughter Anna, who lived here until 1982.

12.00–17.00 Weds–Sun (other times by appointment).
£++ Concessions S G
⊖ Finchley Rd
🚆 Finchley Rd & Frognal
🚌 13, 46, 82, 113, 268, C11, C12

Name of Governing Body:
Freud Museum Trust
Independent
freud@ GN.APC.ORG
£4½2

Florence Nightingale Museum

would like us to email the results to him if we correlate the figures in some way

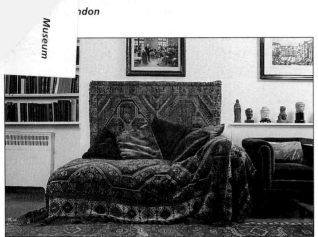

Freud's psychoanalytic couch,
Freud Museum

⊖ London Bridge
≋ London Bridge
🚌 17, 21, 22A, 35, 40, 43, 47, 48, 133, 344, 501, 521, 705, D1, D11, P3, P11, X43

Name of Governing Body:
United Medical and Dental Schools
Independent

GEFFRYE MUSEUM *[handwritten: NANCY CORDER @ ½ hr 14·0030 emailing]*

Kingsland Road
London E2 8EA
☎ 0171-739 9893

These early 18th-century almshouses contain a series of period room reconstructions telling the story of popular furniture and furnishing in Britain. There is also a delightful walled herb garden open from April to October.

10.00–17.00 Tues–Sat,
14.00–17.00 Sun & Bank Hol Mons.
£ Free   W   G   📖
⊖ Old St, Liverpool St, then bus
≋ Old St, Liverpool St
🚌 22A, 22B, 67, 149, 243

Name of Governing Body:
Geffrye Museum Trust
Independent

GILLETTE UK LTD

Great West Road
Isleworth
Middlesex TW7 5NP
☎ 0181-560 1234 ext 7554

A collection of company archives and items relating to the history of shaving.

Open for research by appointment.
£ Free
⊖ Osterley
🚌 H91

Name of Governing Body:
Gillette UK Ltd
Independent

GORDON MUSEUM

UMDS (Guy's Campus)
London SE1 9RT
☎ 0171-955 4358

Major collection of pathological, anatomical and dermatological material used in the teaching of medicine and a small collection of historical artefacts associated with the history of Guy's Hospital.

09.00–17.00 Mon–Fri by appointment to people associated with the medical profession.
£ Free

GOVERNMENT ART COLLECTION

c/o Department of National Heritage
2–4 Cockspur Street
London SW1Y 5DH *[handwritten: WRONG]*
☎ 0171-287 2877 *[handwritten: NUMBER]*

One of the largest holdings of British art from all periods. Many of the works are on loan to British government buildings at home and abroad.

Open for research by appointment
£ Free
⊖ Embankment
≋ Charing Cross
🚌 3, 6, 9, 11, 12, 13, 15, 23, 24, 29, 53, 77A, 88, 91, 94, 109, 139, 159, 176, X15, X53

Name of Governing Body:
HM Government
National

GRANGE MUSEUM OF COMMUNITY HISTORY

On Neasden Roundabout
Neasden Lane
London NW10 1QB
☎ 0181-452 8311

This converted 18th-century stableblock contains displays which show how life in the borough has changed through the 20th century and which reflect the multicultural nature of the local area. Special features include a gallery for exhibitions by the local community and replicas of period rooms, including a Victorian parlour.

Sept–May, 11.00–17.00 Mon–Fri, 10.00–17.00 Sat. June–Aug, 11.00–17.00 Tues–Fri, 10.00–17.00 Sat, 14.00–17.00 Sun.
£ Free   S   G   Ⅴ   P
⊖ Neasden
🚌 16, 112, 182, 245, 297, 302

Name of Governing Body:
London Borough of Brent
Local Authority

GREAT ORMOND STREET HOSPITAL FOR CHILDREN

Peter Pan Gallery
55 Great Ormond Street
London WC1N 3JH
☎ 0171-405 9200 ext 5920/5701

The Peter Pan Gallery contains a small exhibition on the history of the Great Ormond Street Hospital, from its founding in 1852, and a collection of letters and articles written by Charles Dickens and James Barrie in support of the hospital.

Open by appointment.
£ Free
⊖ Russell Sq, Holborn
≳ King's Cross, Euston
🚌 7, 8, 19, 22B, 25, 38, 55, 68, 91, 168, 188, 501, 505, X68

Name of Governing Body:
Great Ormond Street Hospital for Children NHS Trust
Independent

GREENWICH BOROUGH MUSEUM

232 Plumstead High Street
London SE18 1JT
☎ 0181-855 3240

Grange Museum of Community History

The museum mounts exhibitions of archaeology, social history and natural history relating to Greenwich, Woolwich, Eltham, Deptford, Charlton, Plumstead and the new town of Thamesmead. There is also a programme of temporary exhibitions and holiday activities and a Saturday Club.

14.00–19.00 Mon, 10.00–13.00 & 14.00–17.00 Tues & Thurs–Sat. Closed Sun & Wed.
£ Free   S
≳ Plumstead
🚌 96, 99, 180, 272, 422, 464

Name of Governing Body:
London Borough of Greenwich
Local Authority

GUARDS MUSEUM

Wellington Barracks
Birdcage Walk
London SW1E 6HQ
☎ 0171-414 3271

A splendid collection of uniforms, weapons and memorabilia illustrating the story of The Queen's Regiments of Foot Guards through their martial history and service to the

Sovereign and the City of London for over three centuries.

10.00–16.00 Sat–Thurs.
£+ Concessions   X   G
⊖ St James's Park
≳ Victoria
🚌 2, 8, 11, 16, 24, 36, 38, 52, 73, 82, 185, 705, C1

Name of Governing Body:
HQ Household Division
Independent

GUILDHALL ART GALLERY

Aldermanbury
London EC2P 2EJ
☎ 0171-332 1632

The gallery exhibits works from the Corporation of London's permanent collection of London topography and Pre-Raphaelite and 19th-century paintings. There is a new permanent gallery planned for September 1997.

Open by appointment.
£ Free
A
⊖ St Paul's, Bank, Moorgate, Mansion House
≳ Moorgate

🚌 4, 8, 11, 15B, 21, 22B, 25, 26, 43, 76, 133, 172, 501, X43

Name of Governing Body:
Corporation of London
Local Authority

GUILDHALL LIBRARY (PRINT ROOM)

Aldermanbury
London EC2P 2EJ
☎ 0171-260 1839 (fax: 0171-600 3384)

The Corporation of London's permanent collection of prints, photographs, drawings, maps, plans, theatre programmes, theatre bills, portraits and other ephemera relating to London.

Gunnersbury Park Museum

09.30–17.00 Mon–Fri
£ Free   X
⊖ St. Paul's, Moorgate, Bank
⇌ Moorgate, Liverpool St
🚌 4, 8, 11, 15B, 21, 22B, 25, 26, 43, 76, 133, 172, 501, X43

Name of Governing Body:
Corporation of London
Local Authority

GUINNESS ARCHIVES

Hop Store No. 2
Park Royal Brewery
Park Royal
London NW10 7RR
☎ 0181-965 7700 ext 3975

This company museum holds statutory and business records, together with advertising material and artefacts relating to Guinness.

Open for research by appointment.
£ Free   P
⊖ Park Royal, Hanger Lane
🚌 83, 112, 187, 224, 226, PR1, PR2

Name of Governing Body:
Guinness Brewing Worldwide Ltd
Independent

GUNNERSBURY PARK MUSEUM

Gunnersbury Park
London W3 8LQ
☎ 0181-992 1612 (fax: 0181-752 0686)

This local history museum for Ealing and Hounslow is set in a splendid mansion, home of the Rothschild family until 1925. Displays include costume, carriages and temporary exhibitions. The original Victorian kitchens are also open on summer weekends.

Apr–Oct, 13.00–17.00 Mon–Fri, 13.00–18.00 Sat, Sun & Bank Hols. Nov–Mar, 13.00–16.00 Daily. Closed some Public Hols.
£ Free   A   G   🍴   X   P
⊖ Acton Town
⇌ Gunnersbury
🚌 E3 (Daily), 7 (Sun)

Name of Governing Body:
London Borough of Hounslow (on behalf of the London Boroughs of Ealing and Hounslow)
Local Authority

HACKNEY MUSEUM *been closed 4 yrs open again in April!*

Central Hall
Mare Street
London E8 1HE
☎ 0181-986 6914

The museum houses displays of social history and the visual arts, concentrating on the history of Hackney and the worldwide roots of Hackney people. There is also a lively programme of temporary exhibitions.

10.30–12.30 & 13.30–17.00 Tues–Fri, 13.30–17.00 Sat.
£ Free   W   G
⇌ Hackney Central
🚌 22A, 22B, 30, 38, 48, 55, 106, 236, 253, 277, D6, W15

Name of Governing Body:
London Borough of Hackney
Local Authority

HAHNEMANN RELICS

Hahnemann House
2 Powis Place
Great Ormond Street
London WC1N 3HT
☎ 0171-837 9469

A small display of objects relating to Dr Samuel Hahnemann, the founder of homeopathic medicine. The collection includes

Hackney Museum

letters, pictures and some of Dr Hahnemann's personal possessions and original remedies.

Open by appointment only.
£ Free
⊖ Russell Square
≷ Euston, King's Cross
🚍 7, 8, 19, 22B, 25, 38, 55, 68, 77, 77A, 168, 171, 188, 196, 501, 505, X68

Name of Governing Body:
Trustees of Hahnemann House
Independent

HAM HOUSE

Ham Street
Richmond
Surrey TW10 7RS
☎ 0181-940 1950

This sumptuous 17th-century mansion house is still furnished much as it was originally, with painted ceilings, damask and tapestry wall-coverings and ornately carved furniture. Even the fire irons are made of solid silver. The house also contains a collection of rare textiles and several important miniatures, including a portrait of Elizabeth I by Nicholas Hilliard.

Hampstead Museum

Apr–end Oct, 13.00–17.00 Mon–Wed, 13.00–17.30 Sat, 11.30–17.30 Sun. Nov–Dec, 13.00–16.00 Sat & Sun.
£++   X   G   **☕**   **✗**   **🅿**
⊖ Richmond
≷ Richmond
🚍 65, 371

Name of Governing Body:
National Trust
Independent
will phone back

HAMPSTEAD MUSEUM ●

Burgh House
New End Square
London NW3 1LT
☎ 0171-431 0144

A handsome Queen Anne house in the heart of old Hampstead, still with its original panelled

rooms, staircase and wrought-iron gates. Displays investigate the history of the area, and show Hampstead as a fashionable 18th-century spa as well as how the local people coped during the Blitz. There are also exhibitions on Constable and other local artists such as Helen Allingham.

12.00–17.00 Wed–Sun, 14.00–17.00 Bank Hols. Closed Good Friday & 25 Dec.
£ Free   S   A   **☕**   **✗**
⊖ Hampstead
≷ Hampstead Heath
🚍 46, 268, C11

Name of Governing Body:
Burgh House Trust
Independent

HAMPTON COURT PALACE

East Molesey
Surrey KT8 9AU
☎ 0181-977 8441

Henry VIII's riverside palace, built half in Tudor brick and half in Baroque style by Sir Christopher Wren, is set in beautiful gardens and parkland. Within the palace you can view the State Apartments, the Tudor kitchens and the King's Apartments, restored to their former splendour

after the fire of 1986 and brought to life by guides in period costume.

Mid-Mar–mid Oct, 10.15–18.00 Mon, 09.30–18.00 Tues–Sun. Mid-Oct–mid-Mar, 10.15–16.30 Mon, 09.30–16.30 Tues–Sun. Closed 24–26 Dec.
£+++ Concessions   A   G
🍴 ✗ 🅿
🚢 from Richmond, Westminster & Kingston.
🚆 Hampton Court
🚌 111, 131, 216, R68 Green Line 415, 716, 718, 726

Name of Governing Body:
Historic Royal Palaces Agency
National

HARROW MUSEUM AND HERITAGE CENTRE

Headstone Manor
Pinner View
Harrow
Middlesex HA2 6PX
☎ 0181-861 2626

This 14th-century moated manor house and the great tithe barn

house the Whitefriars Glassworks Collection and displays on local history, as well as a series of temporary exhibitions.

12.30–17.00 Wed–Fri, 10.30–17.00 Sat, Sun & Public Hols.
Closes at dusk in winter.
£ Free   W   G   🍴
⊖ Harrow & Wealdstone
🚆 Harrow & Wealdstone
🚌 350, H10, H14, H15, H16

Name of Governing Body:
Harrow Arts Council
Independent

HARROW SCHOOL OLD SPEECH ROOM GALLERY

Church Hill
Harrow on the Hill
Middlesex HA1 3HP
☎ 0181-869 1205
☎ 0181-422 2196

Varied collection of Egyptian, Greek and Roman antiquities, English watercolours, modern British paintings, printed books, Harroviana and natural history.

HMS Belfast

Term time, 14.30–17.00 Daily except Wed. Holidays, 14.30–17.00 Mon–Fri. Please confirm before visiting.
£ Free   S
⊖ Harrow on the Hill, South Harrow
🚆 Harrow on the Hill
🚌 258, H17

Name of Governing Body:
The Keepers and Governors of Harrow School
Independent

HERITAGE CENTRE, HONEYWOOD

Honeywood Walk
Carshalton
Surrey SM5 3NX
☎ 0181-773 4555

Set on the banks of the picturesque town ponds, this listed house contains displays which tell its own story and that of the borough, as well as a changing programme of exhibitions. The house also features a magnificent Edwardian billiards room.

10.00–17.00 Wed–Fri, 10.00–17.30 Sat & Sun.
£+ (free until 13.00) ☕ ✕
🅿
🚋 Carshalton
🚌 127, 154, 157, 407, 408, 413, 726

Name of Governing Body:
London Borough of Sutton
Local Authority

HILLINGDON LOCAL HERITAGE SERVICE

Uxbridge Central Library
High Street
Uxbridge
Middlesex UB8 1HD
☎ 01895-250702

Items from this collection of local historical and archaeological material can be seen on display in the library in a series of temporary exhibitions. There is also an interesting programme of talks, walks and workshops.

Library: 9.30–20.00 Mon, Tues & Thurs; 9.30–17.30 Wed & Fri; 9.30–16.00 Sat.
£ Free
⊖ Uxbridge

Name of Governing Body:
London Borough of Hillingdon
Local Authority

HM TOWER OF LONDON

Tower Hill
London EC3N 4AB
☎ 0171-709 0765

The Tower, begun in the 11th century, has been fortress, treasury, palace and prison. Today it houses the Royal Armouries and the Crown Jewels, as well as a chilling display of torture instruments. You can also view the infamous Traitors' Gate and explore the newly restored medieval palace, where guides in period costume help to recreate the atmosphere of Edward I's reign.

Nov–Feb, 09.30–17.00 Mon–Sat.
Mar–Oct, 09.30–18.00 Mon–Sat, 10.00–18.00 Sun. Last tickets sold one hour before closing.
£+++ Concessions S G ☕
⊖ Tower Hill
🚋 Fenchurch St
🚌 15, 25, 42, 78, 100, D1, D9, D11, X15

Name of Governing Body:
Department of National Heritage
National

HMS BELFAST

Morgan's Lane
(off Tooley Street)
London SE1 2JH
☎ 0171-407 6434

Europe's last surviving big-gun armoured warship to have fought in World War II is now permanently moored close to London Bridge. You can discover how sailors lived on board as you explore all seven decks of this magnificent cruiser.

Mar–Oct, 10.00–18.00 Daily.
Nov–Mar, 10.00–17.00 Daily.
£++ Concessions S ☕
⊖ Monument, London Bridge, Tower Hill, ferry from Tower Hill Pier ➘
🚋 London Bridge
🚌 17, 21, 22A, 35, 40, 43, 47, 48, 133, 344, 501, 521, 705, D1, D11, P3, P11, X43

Name of Governing Body:
Imperial War Museum
National

HOGARTH'S HOUSE

Hogarth Lane
Great West Road
London W4 2QN
☎ 0181-994 6757

This delightful Georgian house, the home of the artist William Hogarth from 1749 to 1764, contains a permanent exhibition of some of his most famous engravings, reproductions of paintings, and memorabilia.

Apr–Sep, 11.00–18.00 Mon–Sat (closed Tues), 14.00–18.00 Sun.
Oct–Mar, 11.00–16.00 Mon–Sat (closed Tues) 14.00–16.00 Sun.
Closed first two weeks of Sept, last three weeks in Dec & New Year's Day.
£ Free S G
⊖ Turnham Green
🚌 27, 190, 237, 267, 290, 391, E3, H40

Name of Governing Body:
London Borough of Hounslow
Local Authority

HORNIMAN MUSEUM AND GARDENS

100 London Road
Forest Hill
London SE23 3PQ
☎ 0181-699 2339 (recorded information)
☎ 0181-699 1872

Important collections of ethnography, musical instruments and natural history illustrating the world we live in – our cultures, arts, crafts, music and natural environment. Displays include an aquarium and the interactive Music Gallery. The museum is set in 16 acres of beautiful gardens and park.

10.30–17.30 Mon–Sat, 14.00–17.30 Sun. Closed 24–26 Dec.
£ Free   E   ☕
⇌ Forest Hill
🚌 63, 122, 171, 176, 185, 312, P4, P13

Name of Governing Body:
Horniman Public Museum & Public Park Trust
Independent

HOUSE OF DETENTION

Clerkenwell Close
London EC1R 0AS
☎ 0171-253 9494

In these underground prison cells, used two centuries ago, are displays charting 300 years of crime and punishment. The collection includes prison records, medical instruments, punishment devices and the equipment used by England's last official hangman.

Imperial War Museum

10.00–18.00 daily. Closed 25 Dec.
£++ Concessions
⊖ Farringdon
🚌 19, 38, 171A

Name of Governing Body:
House of Detention Ltd
Independent

HUNTERIAN MUSEUM

See Museums of the Royal College of Surgeons of England

IMPERIAL WAR MUSEUM

Lambeth Road
London SE1 6HZ
☎ 0171-416 5000,
☎ 0171-820 1683 (recorded information)

National collection documenting the two world wars and other 20th century military operations involving Britain and the Commonwealth. Includes the Blitz experience, the Trench experience and Operation Jericho.

10.00–18.00 Daily. Closed 24–26 Dec.
£+++ Concessions   X   G   Ⅴ
✗
⊖ Lambeth North, Elephant & Castle
⇌ Waterloo
🚌 3, 12, 45, 53, 63, 68, 109, 159, 168, 171, 176, 188, 344, C10

Name of Governing Body:
Trustees of the Imperial War Museum
National

INNS OF COURT AND CITY YEOMANRY MUSEUM

10 Stone Buildings
Lincoln's Inn Fields
London WC2A 3TG
☎ 0171-405 8112

Island History Trust

Small collection of uniforms, equipment, medals, prints, etc. of the Inns of Court Regiments and the City of London Yeomanry (the Rough Riders) during the period from 1798 to the present day.

Tues, by appointment only.
£ Free
⊖ Chancery Lane
🚌 8, 22B, 25, 55, 68, 91, 168, 171, 188, 501, 505, 521

Name of Governing Body:
Inns of Court and City Yeomanry Museum Trust
Independent

Institution of Mechanical Engineers

1 Birdcage Walk
London SW1H 9JJ
☎ 0171-222 7899

Library, archives and collection of engineering objects and models from the Great Exhibition of 1851 to the present day.

09.15–17.30 by appointment only.
£ Free S
⊖ St James's Park, Westminster
⇌ Victoria
🚌 3, 11, 12, 24, 53, 77A, 88, 109, 159, 211, 705, S1, S2, X2, X3, X53

Name of Governing Body:
Institution of Mechanical Engineers
Independent

Island History Trust

Island House
Roserton Street
London E14 3PG
☎ 0171-987 6041

Large collection of photographs illustrating family and community

life on the Isle of Dogs from the 1880's to 1980's.

13.30–16.30 Tues, Wed & Fri.
£ Free S G X
Crossharbour
🚌 277, D1, D5, D6, D7, D8, D9, P14

Name of Governing Body:
Island History Trust
Independent

Islington Museum Gallery

268 Upper Street
Islington
London N1 2UQ
☎ 0171-354 9442,
☎ ~~0171-477 3851~~ (administration)

This gallery is the venue for a lively programme of temporary exhibitions on themes related to the Borough of Islington. They cover fine and applied arts, local history and the environment.

11.00–15.00 Wed–Sat,
12.00–16.00 Sun.
£ Free
⊖ Highbury & Islington
⇌ Highbury & Islington
🚌 4, 19, 30, 43, 153, 236, 271, 277, 279, X43

Name of Governing Body:
London Borough of Islington
Local Authority

IVEAGH BEQUEST, KENWOOD

Hampstead Lane
London NW3 7JR
☎ 0181-348 1286

This mansion, on the borders of Hampstead Heath, is a fine example of the work of designer and architect Robert Adams, who remodelled Kenwood from 1764-73. Much of the interior, including the magnificent library, was also designed by him. The house contains the Iveagh Bequest of Old Master and British paintings, including works by Rembrandt, Vermeer, Frans Hals, Turner, Gainsborough and Reynolds.

1 Oct–31 Mar, 10.00–16.00. 1 April–30 Sept, 10.00–18.00. Closed 24 & 25 Dec.
£ Free   W   G   🍽   ✕
⊖ Archway or Golders Green, then 210 bus
🚌 210

Name of Governing Body:
English Heritage
Nationally funded

JEWISH MUSEUM

Raymond Burton House
129–131 Albert Street
London NW1 7NB
☎ 0171-284 1997

Amalgamated with the London Museum of Jewish Life on a two-site basis, this museum houses a collection of ceremonial art, antiquities and portraits, illustrating Jewish life, history and religion. Audio-visual programmes explain Jewish festivals and ceremonies.

10.00–16.00 Sun–Thurs. Closed Fri, Sat, Public Hols & Jewish festivals.
£++ Concessions   W

⊖ Camden Town
≋ Camden Rd
🚌 274, C2

Name of Governing Body:
The Jewish Museum
Independent

LONDON MUSEUM OF JEWISH LIFE

The Sternberg Centre
80 East End Road
Finchley
London N3 2SY
☎ 0181-349 1143

The London Museum of Jewish Life focuses on the social history of Jewish London and of Jewish people now living in Britain. Its collections include documents, photographs and oral history archives and it also runs educational programmes, guided walks and travelling exhibitions for loan to museums and other organisations.

10.30–17.00 Mon–Thurs, 10.30–16.30 Sun (except Aug & Bank Hol weekends). Closed

Iveagh Bequest, Kenwood House

Jewish festivals, Public Hols & 24 Dec–4 Jan.
£ Varies subject to exhibition
🍽 12–13.30 Mon–Thur   X   G
⊖ Finchley Central
🚌 13, 82, 112, 143, 260

Name of Governing Body:
Trustees of the London Museum of Jewish Life
Independent

MicK ScOTT
7332 3823

KEATS HOUSE

Keats Grove
Hampstead
London NW3 2RR
☎ 071-435 2062

This furnished Regency house, once the home of the poet John Keats, contains letters, books and relics of Keats, his circle and family. The Keats Memorial Library (8, 600 volumes) and the Kate Greenaway collection may be viewed by appointment only.

Apr–Oct, 10.00–13.00 & 14.00–18.00 Mon–Fri,
will phone back

10.00–13.00 & 14.00–17.00 Sat,
14.00–17.00 Sun & Bank Hols.
Nov–Mar, 13.00–17.00 Mon–Fri,
Sat & Sun as Apr–Oct. Closed
24–26 Dec, 1 Jan, Good Friday,
Easter Eve & May Day.
£ Free   S   G
⊖ Hampstead, Belsize Park
⇌ Hampstead Heath
🚌 24, 46, 168, 268, C11

Name of Governing Body:
London Borough of Camden
Local Authority

**KENSINGTON PALACE, STATE
APARTMENTS & ROYAL
CEREMONIAL DRESS
COLLECTION**

Kensington Palace
London W8 4PX
☎ 0171-937 9561

Much of Kensington Palace still
serves as a London residence for
members of the Royal Family, but
the sumptuous state apartments,
designed by Sir Christopher Wren

and occupied at various times by
William III and Queen Mary II,
George I and George II, are open
to the public. The rooms below
hold a dazzling display of royal
ceremonial dress spanning the
reigns of 12 monarchs.

Restoration work being
undertaken. Open from Apr to
Sept, please call to confirm hours.
£+++ Concessions   S   G   🍵
✗
⊖ Notting Hill Gate, Queensway,
High Street Kensington
🚌 9, 9A, 10, 27, 28, 31, 49, 52,
70, 415, 702, 740

Name of Governing Body:
Historic Royal Palaces
National

**KEW BRIDGE STEAM
MUSEUM**

Green Dragon Lane
Brentford
Middlesex TW8 OEN
☎ 0181-568 4757

*Jewish
Museum*

The five vast steam engines in this
former Victorian waterworks once
pumped drinking water to houses
in west London. Three of these
have now been fully restored and
at weekends you can see them
pumping away. There is also an
exhibition on the history of
London's water supply, including a
water main made out of hollowed
tree trunks.

11.00–17.00 Daily. In steam at
weekends only.
£++ Concessions (weekend),
+ Concessions (weekday)   X   G
🍵 Weekends only
⊖ Gunnersbury
⇌ Kew Bridge
🚌 7, 65, 237, 267, 391

Name of Governing Body:
**Kew Bridge Engines Trust &
Water Supply Museum Ltd**
Independent

**KEW COLLECTIONS OF
ECONOMIC BOTANY**

Royal Botanic Gardens
Kew
Richmond
Surrey TW9 3AB
☎ 0181-940 1171

This vast collection is composed of
73, 000 different items derived
from plants, including foods,
beverages, fibres, fabrics, paper
dyes, medicinal compounds,
gums, resins, rubber and timber
which have been put to economic
use by people from all parts of
the world.

Open to researchers by
appointment.
£++ Concessions (includes entry
to Kew Gardens and two
galleries)   🍵   X   🅿
⊖ Kew Gardens
⇌ Kew Bridge
🚌 65, 391

Name of Governing Body:
Trustees of the Royal Botanic Gardens, Kew
National

KEW GARDENS GALLERY
Royal Botanic Gardens
Kew
Richmond
Surrey TW9 3AB
☎ 0181-332 5618

The gallery mounts changing exhibitions of contemporary and historical flower paintings and botanical illustrations. A number of the exhibitions include paintings for sale.

09.30 to dusk Daily. Closed 25 Dec & 1 Jan.
£++ Concessions (includes entry to Kew Gardens and Marianne North Gallery) 🍴 ✗ 🅿
⊖ Kew Gardens
⇌ Kew Bridge
🚌 65, 391, 267

Kingston Museum

Name of Governing Body:
Trustees of the Royal Botanic Gardens, Kew
National

KEW PALACE & QUEEN CHARLOTTE'S COTTAGE
Royal Botanic Gardens
Kew
Richmond
Surrey TW9 3AB
☎ 0181-940 1171

Built in 1631, the palace reflects the private lifestyle of George III and Queen Charlotte, who used it as their family retreat. It is set idyllically in the Royal Botanic Gardens.

Apr–end Sept, 11.00–17.30.
£+ W G 🍴 ✗ 🅿
⊖ Kew Gardens
⇌ Kew Gardens, Kew Bridge
🚌 65, 391

Name of Governing Body:
Historic Royal Palaces Agency
National

KINGSTON MUSEUM
Wheatfield Way
Kingston-upon-Thames
Surrey KT1 2PS
☎ 0181-546 5386

Displays tell the story of Kingston upon Thames. The newly restored first-floor art gallery houses temporary exhibitions of arts, crafts, photography and local history.

10.00–17.00 Mon, Tues & Thurs–Sat.
£ Free 🅿
⇌ Kingston
🚌 57, 65, 85, 131, 213, 371, 431, K5, K9, K10

Name of Governing Body:
Royal Borough of Kingston upon Thames
Local Authority

KIRKALDY TESTING MUSEUM
99 Southwark Street
Southwark
London SE1 OJF
☎ 01322-332195

Housed in this purpose-built structure of 1874 is the original all-purpose materials testing machine designed by David Kirkaldy (1820–1897). With this machine and others the museum aims to demonstrate the standardisation of materials testing developed by David Kirkaldy and the long history of the family works.

Open by appointment only.
£++ Concessions
⊖ London Bridge
⇌ London Bridge
🚌 17, 21, 22A, 35, 40, 43, 47, 48, 133, 149, 344, 501, 521, D1, D11, P11, X43

Name of Governing Body:
The Kirkaldy Museum Trust Ltd
Independent

will phone back

2 0200 00
4.5°

LEIGHTON HOUSE MUSEUM

12 Holland Park Road
London W14 8LZ
☎ 0171-602 3316

This flamboyant studio house was purpose-built for the Victorian painter, Lord Leighton, and contains a spectacular Arab Hall lined with 16th- and 17th-century Isnik tiles. The house also holds collections of furniture, ceramics and paintings by Leighton and his contemporaries.

11.00–17.30 Mon–Sat. Closed Sun and Public Hols.
£ Free   W   G
⊖ High Street Kensington
🚌 9, 9A, 10, 27, 28, 49

Name of Governing Body:
Royal Borough of Kensington and Chelsea
Local Authority

LIBRARY AND MUSEUM OF THE UNITED GRAND LODGE OF ENGLAND

Freemasons' Hall
Great Queen Street
London WC2B 5AZ
☎ 0171-831 9811

Freemasons' Hall, the headquarters of the United Grand Lodge of England, houses a riveting exhibition on the history of Freemasonry in Britain, from its origins in the 16th century. The museum's displays include Masonic regalia and jewels, portraits and items that have been used for Masonic purposes or have Masonic decoration.

10.00–17.00 Mon–Fri,
10.00–13.00 Sat. Closed Public Hols and preceeding Sat.
£ Free   X   G
⊖ Covent Garden, Holborn
🚌 1, 8, 19, 22B, 25, 38, 55, 68,

91, 98, 168, 171, 188, 501, 505, 521, X68

Name of Governing Body:
United Grand Lodge of Free and Accepted Masons of England
Independent

LINLEY SAMBOURNE HOUSE

18 Stafford Terrace
London W8 7BH
☎ 0181-994 1019

This Victorian town house, superbly preserved with its original decorations, fixtures and furniture, was the home of *Punch* illustrator Linley Sambourne (1844–1910). It is a unique example of a successful artist's house in 'artistic' Kensington.

Mar-Oct, 10.00–16.00 Wed, 14.00–17.00 Sun.

Leighton House Museum

£++ Concessions   S
⊖ High Street Kensington
🚌 9, 9A, 10, 27, 28, 31, 49, 52, 70, C1,

Name of Governing Body:
Royal Borough of Kensington and Chelsea (administrated by the Victorian Society)
Independent

LITTLE HOLLAND HOUSE

40 Beeches Avenue
Carshalton
Surrey SM5 3LW
☎ 0181-770 4781
☎ 0181-773 4555

Home of Frank Dickinson (1874–1961) artist, designer and craftsman, inspired by William

Morris and John Ruskin. The Grade II listed interior features paintings, hand-made furniture and craft objects.

13.30–17.30 first Sun of each month & Sun & Mon of Bank Hol weekends. Closed 25 Dec & 1 Jan.
£ Free
⊖ Morden
⇌ Carshalton Beeches
🚌 154

Name of Governing Body:
London Borough of Sutton
Local Authority

Livesey Museum

682 Old Kent Road
London SE15 1JF
☎ 0171-639 5604
☎ 0171-277 5384 (recorded information)

One of London's most lively museums, the Livesey has a programme of temporary 'hands-on' exhibitions aimed at families and children. The museum has no permanent collection, but borrows objects from other Southwark museums to create innovative and

Livesey Museum

interactive displays and exhibitions on topical issues, such as 'The Great Rubbish Show'.

10.00–17.00 Mon–Sat
£ Free   A G 🅿
⊖ Elephant & Castle, then bus
⇌ Elephant & Castle/Queen's Rd, then bus
🚌 21, 53, 78, 172, P11, P13

Name of Governing Body:
London Borough of Southwark
Local Authority

£600   2.50 1.25

London Canal Museum

12/13 New Wharf Road
King's Cross
London N1 9RT
☎ 0171-713 0836

Located in a former Victorian ice-house are displays which tell the story of London's waterways, from their days as an important trade route to their current use for more leisurely pursuits. You can also view the vast ice-well underneath the museum, where ice imported from Norway was once stored to make ice-cream.

10.00–16.30 Tues–Sun. Last admission 15.45. Open Bank Hols.
£++ Concessions   S
⊖ King's Cross
⇌ King's Cross, St Pancras
🚌 10, 17, 18, 30, 45, 46, 63, 73, 91, 214, 221, 259, C12

Name of Governing Body:
Canal Museum Trust
Independent

London Chest Hospital

Bonner Road
London E2 9JX
☎ 0181-980 4433

The hospital houses the Capel Collection of historic medical and surgical instruments. These include a 'Lister carbolic spray' said to be the one that Lister himself used.

Open by written appointment.
£ Free   Ⓥ
⊖ Bethnal Green
⇌ Cambridge Heath
🚌 8, 26, 48, 55, 106, 253, 309, D6

Name of Governing Body:
The Royal Hospitals NHS Trust
Independent

London Fire Brigade Museum

Winchester House
94a Southwark Bridge Road
London SE1 OEG
☎ 0171-587 2894

The history of firefighting, from the Great Fire of London in 1666 to the present day, is outlined in this museum. The exhibits include some of the pumps and engines that were used and there are displays on the origins of the first London Fire Engine Establishment and how the fire brigade coped during the Blitz.

Guided tours by appointment only.
£++ Concessions   S
⊖ Borough
⇌ London Bridge
🚌 21, 35, 40, 133, 149, 344, D1, D11, P3, P11

Name of Governing Body:
LFCDA
Independent

LONDON GAS MUSEUM

North Thames Gas
Twelvetrees Crescent ·
Bromley-by-Bow
London E3 3JH
☎ 0171-987 2000 ext 3344

This private museum tells the history of the gas industry, from its pioneering beginnings in the 19th century to the present day. The displays, including replicas of period rooms, show how technological developments changed people's lives. There is also a collection of gas artefacts including gas cookers, fires, fridges and even a gas-powered radio.

09.00–16.00 Mon–Fri, by appointment. Open evenings & weekends by appointment to groups (charge).
£ Free   S   🅿
⊖ Bromley-by-Bow
🚌 108, S2

Name of Governing Body:
British Gas Plc
Independent

LONDON IRISH RIFLES

Duke of York's HQ
Kings Road, Chelsea
London SW3 4SA
☎ 0171-930 4466 ext 5406

A collection of items and important documents relating to the history of the London Irish Rifles (TA) from the year of their formation, 1859.

Open by appointment.
£ Free
⊖ Sloane Square
⇌ Victoria
🚌 11, 19, 22, 137, 137A, 211, 249, 319, C1

Name of Governing Body:
London Irish Rifles Regimental Association
Independent

LONDON MUSEUM OF JEWISH LIFE

see Jewish Museum

LONDON SCOTTISH REGIMENTAL MUSEUM

95 Horseferry Road
London SW1P 2DX
☎ 0171-630 1639

The museum tells the history of the London Scottish Regiment through displays of artefacts, documents and a colourful selection of uniforms.

By appointment only.
£ Free
⊖ St James's Park
⇌ Victoria
🚌 11, 24, 88, 211, 507, C10

Name of Governing Body:
The London Scottish Regimental Trust
Independent

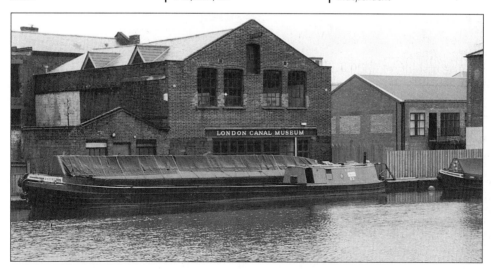

LONDON TOY AND MODEL MUSEUM

21–23 Craven Hill
London W2 3EN
☎ 0171-706 8000 *closed down*

Re-opened in Spring 1995 after extensive redevelopment, the museum houses a huge collection of toys and working models arranged in twenty themed galleries including an Aerodrome, a Penny Arcade and a room for futuristic toy robots and spaceships. The toys date mostly from the 19th and 20th centuries, but the collection includes a clay model of a Roman gladiator made in the 1st century A.D.

10.00–17.30 Mon–Sat,
11.00–17.30 Sun & Bank Hols.
£+++ Concessions S ▼ ✗
⊖ Queensway, Bayswater,
Lancaster Gate
⇌ Paddington
🚌 12, 70, 94, 290

Name of Governing Body:
The Toy Museum Ltd
Independent

LONDON TRANSPORT MUSEUM

Covent Garden
London WC2E 7BB
☎ 0171-379 6344
☎ 0171-836 8557 (recorded information)

The story since 1800 of the world's largest urban passenger transport system and its impact on the growth of London and its suburbs, illustrated by interactive exhibits, video displays, posters, models and photographs.

10.00–18.00 Sat–Thurs.
11.00–18.00 Fri.
£+++ Concessions W G ▼
⊖ Covent Garden, Leicester Sq,
Holborn

⇌ Charing Cross, Waterloo
🚌 6, 9, 11, 15, 23, 26

Name of Governing Body:
London Regional Transport
Independent

MARBLE HILL HOUSE

Richmond Road
Twickenham
Middlesex TW1 2NL
☎ 0181-892 5115

This Palladian villa by the Thames was built in 1724–1729 for Henrietta Howard, mistress of George II, and is now furnished with paintings and furniture of the period, including works by Hayman, Gravelot, Reynolds, Wilson and Panini. The Lazenby Bequest chinoiserie collection is also on display.

1 Apr–31 Oct, 10.00–13.00 & 14.00–18.00 Daily. 1 Nov–31 Mar, 10.00–16.00 Wed–Sun. Closed 24–26 Dec & 1 Jan.
£+ Concessions A ✗ 🅿
⊖ Richmond

London Transport Museum

⇌ St Margaret's, Richmond
🚌 33, 90, 290, H22, R68, R70

Name of Governing Body:
English Heritage
Nationally funded

MARIANNE NORTH GALLERY

Royal Botanic Gardens
Richmond
Kew
Surrey TW9 3AB
☎ 0181-332 5621

A beautiful collection of brightly coloured paintings of flowers, insects, birds and animals, executed by Marianne North. This intrepid Victorian lady travelled round the world painting in the 1870s and 1880s and then established this gallery in which her work was to be displayed.

Telephone for current opening times
£++ Concessions (includes entrance to Kew Gardens,

Marble Hill House

museum and gallery) S ☕ ✗
🅿
⊖ Kew Gardens
≋ Kew Gardens, Kew Bridge, Richmond
🚌 65, 391

Name of Governing Body:
Trustees of the Royal Botanic Gardens, Kew
National

MCC MUSEUM
Lord's Ground
St John's Wood
London NW8 8QN
☎ 0171-289 1611 (curator)
☎ 0171-266 3825 (tours dept)

The history of cricket from 1550 to the present day comes to life on a tour of the Long Room and the museum, where you can see portraits of famous cricketers, bats used by the great stroke players and video highlights of outstanding matches.

Guided tours daily 12.00 & 14.00. Guided tours on match days 10.00. Museum open all day match days for ticket holders only.

No tours on Test Match, Cup Final & preparation days.

Guided tours: **£+++** Concessions Museum entrance for ticket holders on match days: **£+** ✗
G ☕ Match days only
⊖ St John's Wood, Marylebone
≋ Marylebone
🚌 13, 43, 82, 113, 139, 274

Name of Governing Body:
Marylebone Cricket Club
Independent

MERTON HERITAGE CENTRE/MUSEUM
The Canons
Madeira Road
Surrey CR4 4HD
☎ 0181-640 9387

This newly opened museum has a programme of temporary exhibitions on themes related to local history. The objects on display are borrowed from other museums, history societies and local people and many of them can be handled by visitors.

10.00–17.00 Fri & Sat. At other times by appointment.
£ Free ✗ 🅿
⊖ Morden, then 118 bus

≋ Mitcham
🚌 118, 200, 270, 280, 355

Name of Governing Body:
London Borough of Merton
Local Authority

METROPOLITAN POLICE THAMES DIVISION MUSEUM
TDHQ
Wapping Police Station
98 Wapping High Street
London E1 9NE
☎ 0171-275 4465

This police station holds a wide variety of material relating to the history of the Metropolitan Police Thames Division (the River Police).

Open by written appointment.
£ Free
⊖ Tower Hill, Wapping
🚌 100

Name of Governing Body:
Metropolitan Police Museum Trust
Independent

MICHAEL FARADAY'S LABORATORY AND MUSEUM (ROYAL INSTITUTION)
Royal Institution of Great Britain
21 Albemarle Street
London W1X 4BS
☎ 0171-409 2992

Restored laboratory where Faraday made some of his most important discoveries in the fields of magnetism and electricity and the links between the two. Some of the laboratory's original apparatus is on show, together with manuscripts and Faraday personalia.

13.00–16.00 Mon–Fri except Public Hols. Parties & conducted tours by appointment.
£+ Concessions ✗ G

Green Park
8, 9, 14, 19, 22, 38

Name of Governing Body:
The Royal Institution of Great Britian
Independent

MUSEUM OF ARTILLERY IN THE ROTUNDA

Repository Road
Woolwich
London SE18
☎ 0181-781 3127
☎ 0181-316 5402

Traces the development of the gun from medieval days until the present time. The displays are housed in an early 19th century 'tent' designed by John Nash.

13.00–16.00 Mon–Fri. Closed weekends & Public Hols
£ Free   X   G   Ⓥ   Ⓟ
⇌ Woolwich Arsenal, Woolwich Dockyard
🚌 53, 54, 380, X53

Name of Governing Body:
Royal Artillery Institution
Independent

MUSEUM OF FULHAM PALACE

Fulham Palace
Bishops Avenue
London SW6 6EA
☎ 0171-736 3233

This Tudor manor house, with Georgian additions, was once the residence of the Bishop of London. The museum has displays on the history of the building, its gardens and the bishops who lived in it.

Mar–Oct, 14.00–17.00 Wed–Sun.
Nov–Feb, 13.00–16.00 Wed–Sun.

Museum of London

Group tours with refreshments by appointment. Grounds and herb garden open daily.
£+ Concessions
⊖ Putney Bridge
⇌ Putney
🚌 14, 22, 39, 74, 85, 93, 220, 265, 270, 718, 740, C4

Name of Governing Body:
Fulham Palace Trust
Independent

MUSEUM OF GARDEN HISTORY

The Tradescant Trust
Lambeth Palace Road
London SE1 7LB
☎ 0171-261 1891

Situated in the historic church of St Mary at Lambeth, this museum celebrates the work of the two John Tradescants, father and son, who brought home from their travels many of the plants we know today. Part of the churchyard has been designed as a replica of a 17th century garden and the museum hosts a variety of temporary exhibitions and events.

10.30–16.00 Mon–Fri,
10.30–17.00 Sun. Closed Sat.
£ Free   X   G   🍵   ✗

⊖ Waterloo, Lambeth North
⇌ Waterloo
🚌 3, 77, 159, 344, 507, C10

Name of Governing Body:
The Tradescant Trust
Independent
w.il ?.b.

MUSEUM OF LONDON

London Wall
London EC2Y 5HN
☎ 0171-600 3699

Tells the fascinating story of the capital from prehistoric times to the 20th-century. Highlights include a Roman kitchen, a sparkling collection of Elizabethan jewellery, a formidable 18th-century prison cell, and the sumptuous Lord Mayor's coach.

10.00–17.50 Tues–Sat & Bank Hols, 12.00–17.50 Sun.
£++ Concessions   W   E   G
🍵   ✗
⊖ Moorgate, Barbican, St Paul's
⇌ Moorgate, St Paul's Thameslink
🚌 4, 8, 11, 15, 22B, 23, 25, 141, 172, 501, 521

Name of Governing Body:
Board of Governors of the Museum of London
Local Authority/Centrally funded

Museum of the Moving Image
no answer

MUSEUM OF MANKIND

(The Ethnography Department of
the British Museum)
6 Burlington Gardens
London W1X 2EX
☎ 0171-323 8043 (information)

Changing exhibitions illustrating
the variety of non-Western
cultures. These include the
indigenous peoples of Africa,
Australia and the Pacific Islands,
North and South America and
certain parts of Asia and Europe.

10.00–17.00 Mon–Sat,
14.30–18.00 Sun.
£ Free X G 🍵
⊖ Green Park, Piccadilly Circus,
Oxford Circus
⇌
🚌 3, 6, 9, 12, 13, 14, 15, 19, 22,
23, 38, 53, 88, 94, 139, 159, X53

Name of Governing Body:
British Museum
National *k about 11,000 per annum*

MUSEUM OF RICHMOND

Old Town Hall
Whittaker Avenue
Richmond
Surrey TW9 1TP
☎ 0181-332 1141

The history of Richmond, Kew,
Petersham and Ham is told in a
lively and informative way
through displays, models and
audio-visual programmes.

May–Oct, 11.00–17.00 Tues–Sat,
14.00–17.00 Sun. Nov–Apr,
11.00–17.00 Tues–Sat.
£+ Concessions W
⊖ Richmond
⇌ Richmond
🚌 33, 65, 90, 190, 290, 337,
371, 391, R68, R70

Name of Governing Body:
The Museum of Richmond
Independent
£2
£1/conc children free

MUSEUM OF THE HONOURABLE ARTILLERY COMPANY

Armoury House
City Road
London EC1Y 2BQ
☎ 0171-382 1537

History of the Company from the
16th century, illustrated through
uniforms, weapons, equipment,
applied art, silver and medals.

Open by appointment only
£ Free
⊖ Old St, Moorgate
⇌ Moorgate, Liverpool St
🚌 21, 43, 76, 141, 214, 271, X43

Name of Governing Body:
Honourable Artillery Company
Independent

MUSEUM OF THE MOVING IMAGE *CLOSED*

South Bank
Waterloo
London SE1 8XT
☎ 0171-928 3535
(administration)
☎ 0171-401 2636 (recorded
information)

Exciting, informative and fun, the
museum traces the story of the
moving image from early Chinese
Shadow Theatre to film and
television technology, with plenty
of hands-on involvement. There
are also regular changing
exhibitions each year.

10.00–18.00 Daily. Last admission
one hour before closing. Closed
24–26 Dec.
£+++ Concessions W V 🍵
✗
⊖ Waterloo, Embankment
⇌ Waterloo
🚌 1, 4, 26, 68, 76, 77, 149, 168,
171, 171A, 176, 188, 501, 505,
521, D1, D11, P11, X68

Name of Governing Body:
British Film Institute
National

MUSEUM OF THE ORDER OF ST JOHN

St John's Gate
St John's Lane
London EC1M 4DA
☎ 0171-253 6644
not recognised

Collection of artefacts relating to the history of the Order of St John, from its foundation during the crusades in order to care for the sick to the development of the St John Ambulance service. Objects on display range from pharmacy jars and silverware (from which patients were originally fed) to more modern first-aid equipment. The collection is housed in a 16th-century gatehouse and Norman crypt.

10.00–17.00 Mon–Fri, 10.00–16.00 Sat. Closed Sun and Bank Hols. Tours of buildings: 11.00 & 14.30 Tues, Fri, Sat.
£ Free   S
⊖ Farringdon
⇌ King's Cross, Farringdon
🚌 4, 55, 153, 243, 279, 505

Name of Governing Body:
The Order of St John
Independent

MUSEUM OF THE ROYAL PHARMACEUTICAL SOCIETY OF GREAT BRITAIN

1 Lambeth High Street
London SE1 7JN
☎ 0171-735 9141 ext 354

The social and professional history of pharmacy, housed in the headquarters of the Royal Pharmaceutical Society of Great Britain. Displays and a series of temporary exhibitions show representative items from the collection including a fine selection of tin-glazed drug jars, dispensing equipment, prints and photographs.

Museum of the Royal Pharmaceutical Society of Great Britain

09.00–13.00 & 14.00–17.00 by appointment only.
£ Free   A   G
⊖ Vauxhall, Westminster, Lambeth North, Waterloo
⇌ Vauxhall, Waterloo
🚌 3, 3B, 77, 159, 344, 507, C10

Name of Governing Body:
Royal Pharmaceutical Society of Great Britain
Independent

MUSEUM OF ZOOLOGY AND COMPARATIVE ANATOMY

Biology Department (Medawar Building)
University College
Gower Street
London WC1E 6BT
☎ 0171-387 7050 ext 3564

A teaching and research collection of zoological and palaeontological materials of historic and scientific interest.

09.30–17.00 Mon–Fri, closed Bank Hols & for a week at Easter & Christmas. By appointment only.
£ Free   S   🍽   ✗
⊖ Euston Sq, Euston, Goodge St, Warren St
⇌ Euston, King's Cross
🚌 10, 24, 29, 30, 73, 134

Name of Governing Body:
University College London
University

MUSEUMS OF THE ROYAL COLLEGE OF SURGEONS OF ENGLAND

35-43 Lincoln's Inn Fields
London WC2 3PN
☎ 0171-405 3474 ext 3011

The College Museums comprise:
The Hunterian Museum, containing John Hunter's

(1728–1793) collection of comparative and morbid anatomy; *The Odontological Museum*, relating to the scientific study of teeth and the history of Dentistry; *The Wellcome Museum of Pathology* and *The Wellcome Museum of Anatomy*, both including substantial historical and modern specimen and slide collections and surgical instruments.

Hunterian & Odontological Museums: 10.00–17.00 Mon–Fri. Pathology & Anatomy Museums: 09.00–17.00 Mon–Fri. By appointment for members of the medical professions, students, researchers and groups only.
£ Free   A
⊖ Holborn, Temple
🚌 1, 4, 8, 19, 22B, 25, 38, 68, 168, 171A, 188, 501, 505, 521

Name of Governing Body:
The Royal College of Surgeons of England
Independent

no answer

MUSICAL MUSEUM

368 High Street
Brentford
Middlesex TW8 OBD
☎ 0181-560 8108

Museum of Zoology and Comparative Anatomy

An extensive collection of working automatic musical instruments, including everything from a small musical box, to the mighty 'Wurlitzer' theatre organ, all regularly demonstrated.

Apr–Oct, 14.00–17.00 Sat & Sun. Jul–Aug, also 14.00–16.00 Wed–Fri.
£++ Concessions   S   G
⊖ Gunnersbury, South Ealing
≷ Kew Bridge
🚌 7, 65, 237, 267

Name of Governing Body:
The Musical Museum
Independent

NATIONAL ARMY MUSEUM

Royal Hospital Road
London SW3 4HT
☎ 0171-730 0717

Tells the story of the British and Commonwealth soldier from

1485 to the present day. Exhibits include personal relics, weapons, medals, models, equipment, reconstructions and one of the world's finest collections of military uniform.

10.00–17.30 Daily.
£ Free   W   G   Ⓥ   ☕
⊖ Sloane Sq
≷ Victoria
🚌 11, 19, 22, 137, 137A, 211, 239

Name of Governing Body:
The Council of the National Army Museum
National

April to March
£w 778008

NATIONAL GALLERY

Trafalgar Square
London WC2N 5DN
☎ 0171-747 2885

Major collection of Western European paintings dating from the 13th century to the early 20th

£6–8 for special
National Gallery exhibs.

century, including works by Botticelli, Van Eyck, Raphael, Titian, Rembrandt, Canaletto, Constable, Turner, Monet, Renoir and Van Gogh.

10.00–18.00 Mon–Sat, 14.00–18.00 Sun. Also June–Aug 10.00–20.00 Wed.
£ Free W E G

⊖ Charing Cross, Leicester Sq, Piccadilly Circus
≋ Charing Cross
🚌 3, 6, 9, 11, 12, 13, 15, 23, 24, 29, 53, 77A, 88, 91, 94, 109, 139, 159, 176, X15, X53

Name of Governing Body:
Trustees of the National Gallery
National

NATIONAL MARITIME MUSEUM

Romney Road
London SE10 9NF
☎ 0181-858 4422
☎ 0181-293 9618 (recorded information)

Superlative maritime collections tell the history of Britain and the sea. The museum includes models of ships of all ages, full-size vessels and battle paintings.

10.00–17.00 Mon–Sat, 12.00–17.00 Sun.
£+++ Concessions (includes entry to the Old Royal Observatory and the Queen's House) X G ☕
✗
⚓ from Westminster, Charing Cross & Tower piers
≋ Maze Hill   🚤 Island Gardens
🚌 177, 180, 188, 199, 286

Name of Governing Body:
Trustees of the National Maritime Museum
National

NATIONAL MUSEUM OF CARTOON ART

Baird House
15–17 St Cross Street
London EC1N 8UN
☎ 0171-405 4717

Not recognised

The museum is looking for permanent accommodation, but currently mounts a programme of lively temporary exhibitions of humorous and cartoon art from 1750 to the present day.

12.00–18.00 Mon–Fri.
£ Free, but donation requested.
⊖ Farringdon, Chancery Lane
≋ Farringdon
🚌 55, 63, 221, 243, 259, 505

Name of Governing Body:
The Cartoon Art Trust
Independent

NATIONAL PORTRAIT GALLERY

St Martin's Place
London WC2H 0HE
☎ 0171-306 0055

National Maritime Museum

Famous British faces from the Tudors to the present day, depicted in paintings, sculpture, etchings, photographs, miniatures and video films. There is a daily programme of slide lectures, room talks and films for the general public.

10.00–18.00 Mon–Sat. Closed Public Hols.
£ Free S G
⊖ Leicester Sq, Charing Cross
≋ Charing Cross
🚌 3, 6, 9, 11, 12, 13, 15, 23, 24, 29, 53, 77A, 88, 91, 94, 109, 139, 159, 176, 196, X15

Name of Governing Body:
Trustees of the National Portrait Gallery
National

NATIONAL POSTAL MUSEUM

King Edward Building
King Edward Street
London EC1A 1LP
☎ 0171-239 5420

One of the world's greatest collections of postage stamps from around the globe, including designs for British stamps which have never been issued, such as Edward VIII's coronation set.

09.30–16.30 Mon–Fri. Closed
weekends & Public Hols.
£ Free   A   G
⊖ St Paul's, Barbican
⇌ Moorgate
🚌 4, 8, 22B, 25, 172, 501,

Name of Governing Body:
The Post Office
Independent

NATURAL HISTORY MUSEUM

Cromwell Road
London SW7 5BD
☎ 0171-938 9123

Houses a grand total of over 60
million specimens – plants,
animals, fossils, rocks and
minerals. Inside this fine London
landmark, there are hundreds of
exciting, interactive exhibits telling
the story of life on Earth – from
spectacular dinosaurs and
fabulous gems, to a blue whale
the length of a swimming pool.
The Earth Galleries are currently
undergoing major redevelopment
and will open in summer 1996.

10.00–17.50 Mon–Sat,
11.00–17.50 Sun.
£+++ Concessions   G   W   **🍴**
✗
⊖ South Kensington
🚌 14, 45A, 49, 70, 74, C1

Name of Governing Body:
**Trustees of the Natural History
Museum**
National

NELSON COLLECTION, LLOYD'S

1 Lime Street
London EC3M 7HA
☎ 0171-327 6260

A collection of magnificent
swords and silver presentation
pieces given by the Lloyd's
Patriotic Fund (founded 1803) to

Natural History Museum

sea officers, including Nelson, for
acts of gallantry.

By written request only
£ Free   S
⊖ Bank, Monument
⇌ Liverpool St, Cannon St
🚌 15, 25, 40, 100, D1, D9, D11,
X15

Name of Governing Body:
Corporation of Lloyd's
Independent

NORMANSFIELD HOSPITAL THEATRE

Normansfield Hospial
Kingston Road

Teddington
Middlesex TW11 9JH
☎ 0181-977 7583

A remarkably complete and rare
survival of a private entertainment
theatre of the 1870s, still in
working condition.

Open by appointment only.
£ Free   **P**
⇌ Hampton Wick
🚌 281, 285

Name of Governing Body:
**Richmond, Twickenham &
Roehampton Healthcare NHS
Trust**
Independent

North Woolwich Old Station Museum

Pier Road
North Woolwich
London E16 2JJ
☎ 0171-474 7244

This Victorian station by the Woolwich Ferry has indoor and outdoor exhibits, including engines and a reconstructed ticket office, which tell the story of the Great Eastern Railway and the impact of railways on east London's suburbs. The reference collections of local railway material can be studied by appointment.

10.00–17.00 Thurs & Sat.
14.00–17.00 Sun & Bank Hols.
£ Free   X   G
⇌ North Woolwich
🚌 69, 101, 473

Name of Governing Body:
Governors of the Passmore Edwards Museum
Local Authority

Odontological Museum

See Museums of the Royal College of Surgeons of England

Old Operating Theatre, Museum & Herb Garret

9a St Thomas' Street
Southwark
London SE1 9RT
☎ 0171-955 4791

Britain's oldest surviving purpose-built operating theatre is intriguingly situated in the roof space of an elegant 18th-century church. The Garret, once used to store and cure herbs for medicinal use, provides an evocative atmosphere in which to appreciate the displays on medical history, nursing and herbal medicine and to explore the often horrific history of surgery.

10.00–16.00 Tues–Sun & most Mons. Closed 15 Dec–5 Jan.
£+ Concessions   S
θ London Bridge

Old Operating Theatre, Museum & Herb Garret

⇌ London Bridge
🚌 17, 21, 22A, 35, 40, 43, 47, 48, 133, 344, 501, 521, 705, D1, D11, P3, P11, X43

Name of Governing Body:
Lord Brock's Trust
Independent

Old Royal Observatory, Greenwich

Enquiries to National Maritime Museum
☎ 0181-858 4422
☎ 0181 293 9618 (recorded information)

The original home of Greenwich Mean Time, the observatory houses the largest refracting telescope in the UK and a collection of historic timepieces and navigational instruments.

10.00–17.00 Mon–Sat,
12.00–17.00 Sun.
£+++ Concessions (includes entry to the National Maritime Museum and the Queen's House)   S
⚓ from Westminster, Charing Cross & Tower piers to Greenwich Pier
⇌ Maze Hill
🚉 Island Gardens
🚌 53

Name of Governing Body:
Trustees of the National Maritime Museum
National

Oriental and India Office Collections

197 Blackfriars Road
London SE1 8NG
☎ 0171-412 7873

One of the world's most comprehensive collections of

Oriental material relating to the humanities and social sciences, in the languages of Asia and north-east Africa. Also the archives of the East India Company and the India Office, including prints, drawings, maps and private archives.

09.30–17.45 Mon–Fri, 09.30–12.45 Sat.
£ Free 🍵 ✕
⊖ Waterloo, Blackfriars
⇌ Waterloo
🚌 1, 4, 26, 45, 63, 68, 76, 149, 168, 171, 172, 176, 188, 501, 505, 521, D1, D11, P11, X68

Name of Governing Body:
British Library
National

ORLEANS HOUSE GALLERY

Riverside
Twickenham
Middlesex TW1 3DJ
☎ 0181-892 0221

Set in an attractive woodland garden, the baroque Octagon Room (early 18th century) and adjacent art gallery show changing exhibitions of art, crafts, cartoons and paintings from the Ionides Collection of 18th- and 19th-century views of Richmond.

Orleans House Gallery

Apr–Sept, 13.00–17.30 Tues–Sat, 14.00–17.30 Sun & Bank Hols, Oct–Mar, closes at 16.30.
£ Free ✕ G
⇌ St Margaret's, Twickenham
🚌 33, 90, 290, H22, R68, R70

Name of Governing Body:
London Borough of Richmond upon Thames
Local Authority

OSTERLEY PARK HOUSE

Osterley
Middlesex TW7 4RB
☎ 0181-560 3918

Set in 140 acres of landscaped park, Osterley is one of the last great houses with an intact estate in Greater London. The superb

interiors conjure up a vivid of how the well-to-do lived in 18th century.

Apr–Oct, 13.00–17.00 Wed–Sat, 11.00–17.00 Sun & Bank Hols. Closed Good Friday.
£++ Concessions A G 🍵
🅿
⊖ Osterley
🚌 H91

Name of Governing Body:
National Trust
Independent

PERCIVAL DAVID FOUNDATION OF CHINESE ART

53 Gordon Square
London WC1H OPD

Percival David Foundation of Chinese Art

...of Chinese ...a library of ...tern books relating... art and culture. The ceramics, dating from the 10th to the 18th centuries, reflect the tastes of the imperial court and several bear unique dated inscriptions.

10.30–17.00 Mon–Fri. Closed Bank Hols.
£ Free   A   G
⊖ Euston, Euston Sq, Goodge St,

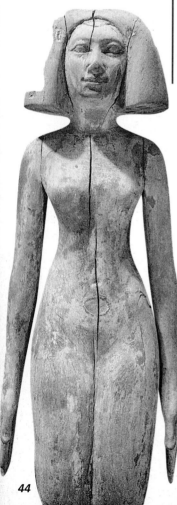

Russell Sq
≋ Euston
🚌 7, 10, 14, 24, 29, 73, 134

Name of Governing Body:
School of Oriental & African Studies, University of London
University
will phone back

PETRIE MUSEUM OF EGYPTIAN ARCHAEOLOGY

University College London
Gower Street
London WC1E 6BT
☎ 0171-387 7050 ext 2884
2076792000
This amazing collection of Egyptian antiquities comes from the excavations of W.M. Flinders Petrie, his colleagues and successors from 1884 to the present day. It is arranged in context to illustrate the development of Egyptian culture, technology and daily life from the Palaeolithic to Roman times.

10.00–12.00 & 13.15–17.00 Mon–Fri. Closed Christmas & Easter weeks, 4 weeks in summer. Occasional Sat opening hours sponsored by the Friends of the Petrie Museum.
£ Free   A   S
⊖ Euston, Warren St, Euston Sq, Russell Sq
≋ Euston
🚌 10, 14, 18, 24, 29, 30, 73, 134

Name of Governing Body:
University College London
University

PITSHANGER MANOR MUSEUM

Mattock Lane
Ealing
London W5 5EQ
☎ 0181-567 1227

The Petrie Museum

Set in an attractive park, Pitshanger Manor was built by the architect John Soane (1753–1837) as his country villa. The house contains a number of rooms furnished in period style and an extensive display of Martinware pottery. The museum also plays host to a series of concerts, workshops and arts events.

10.00–17.00 Tues–Sat.
£ Free   A   G   Ⓥ
⊖ Ealing Broadway
≋ Ealing Broadway
🚌 65, 83, 112, 207, 297, 607, E1, E2, E4, E7, E8, E9, PR1

Name of Governing Body:
London Borough of Ealing
Local Authority Borough
020 84526508

POLISH INSTITUTE AND SIKORSKI MUSEUM

20 Princes Gate
London SW7 1PT
☎ 0171-589 9249
phone back
This vast collection of Polish militaria is the largest outside Poland and includes objects ranging from a vast Turkish tent captured in 1621 to the uniform of General Sikorski, Poland's World War II prime minister and commander-in-chief. The museum also holds a collection of Polish art and a library and historical archive.

14.00–16.00 Mon–Fri. 10.00–16.00 1st Sat of each month.
Other times by appointment for groups.
£ Free   S
⊖ South Kensington, Knightsbridge
🚌 9, 10, 52

Name of Governing Body:
The Polish Institute & Sikorski Museum
Independent

1999   2,000
2000   1,750

POLLOCK'S TOY MUSEUM

1 Scala Street
London W1P 1LT
☎ 0171-636 3452

A delightful collection of toys including dolls, teddy bears, puppets, toy theatres, dolls' houses and folk-toys from around the world. These are housed in an intriguing maze of rooms and narrow winding staircases which is as much fun to explore as the collection itself.

10.00–17.30 Mon–Sat. Closed Bank Hols.
£+ S G
⊖ Goodge St
⇌ Euston
🚌 10, 24, 29, 73, 134

Name of Governing Body:
Trustees of Pollock's Toy Museum
Independent

PRINCE HENRY'S ROOM

17 Fleet Street
London EC4Y 1AA
☎ 0181-294 1158 (fax 0181-294 1084)

Pitshangar Manor Museum

A permanent exhibition of Pepysiana which contains contemporary items, prints and paintings depicting the diarist Samuel Pepys and the London in which he lived.

11.00–14.00 Mon–Sat. Closed Bank Hols.
£ Free   S
⊖ Temple
⇌ Blackfriars
🚌 4, 11, 15, 17A, 23, 26, 76, X15

Name of Governing Body:
Corporation of London
Local Authority

PUBLIC RECORD OFFICE MUSEUM

Chancery Lane
London WC2A 1LR
☎ 0181-878 3666

An exhibition illustrating people and communities from the Middle Ages to the present day, through material in the public records. There are also historically important documents from the national archives, ranging from the Domesday Book to World War II military records.

09.30–17.00 Mon–Fri, closed weekends & Public Hols.
£ Free   S   G   🅿
⊖ Chancery Lane, Temple, Blackfriars
⇌ Blackfriars
🚌 4, 11, 15, 23, 26, 76

Name of Governing Body:
Lord Chancellor's Department
National

PUMPHOUSE EDUCATIONAL MUSEUM

Lavender Pond Nature Park
Lavender Road
Rotherhithe
London SE16 1DZ
☎ 0171-231 2976

Surrounded by a nature park and pond, the museum houses a collection of artefacts found on the Thames foreshore, Peek Frean's ephemera including a replica of Queen Elizabeth's wedding cake and interactive exhibits. It also serves as an environmental study centre for schools.

School terms, 9.30–15.00
Mon–Fri, other times by
appointment.
£ Free, but donation requested
📠
⊖ Rotherhithe, Surrey Quays
🚌 1, 225, P11

Name of Governing Body:
Pumphouse Educational Trust
Independent

PUPPET CENTRE TRUST

BAC
176 Lavender Hill
London SW11 5TN
☎ 0171-228 5335

Nationally important collection of
puppets from all countries and
cultures including the work of
contemporary British puppet
makers.

14.00–18.00 Mon–Fri. At other
times by appointment.
£ Free   W   📠 in Arts Centre
✗
🚃 Clapham Junction
🚌 35, 39, 45A, 77, 77A, 77C,
115, 156, 170, 295, 344, C3, G1

Name of Governing Body:
The Puppet Centre Trust
Independent

QUEEN ELIZABETH'S HUNTING LODGE

Rangers Road
Chingford
London E4 7QH
☎ 0181-529 6681

Much of this Tudor royal
hunting-grandstand has been
restored to its original condition
at the time of Elizabeth I. One of
the floors also houses displays
illustrating the history and uses of
the building.

14.00–17.00 Wed–Sun.
£+ Concessions   S   G   📋
⊖ Walthamstow Central
🚃 Chingford
🚌 97, 97A, 179, 212, 313, 379,
444

Name of Governing Body:
Corporation of London
Local Authority

QUEEN'S GALLERY

Buckingham Palace
London SW1A 1AA
☎ 0171-799 2331 (recorded
information)

Changing exhibitions, drawn from
the huge and diverse Royal
Collection of works of art, which
includes paintings by Canaletto,
Bellini and Vermeer.

9.30–16.30 Daily.
£++ Concessions   S   G
⊖ Victoria, St James's Park, Green
Park
🚃 Victoria
🚌 2, 8, 9, 10, 11, 14, 16, 19, 22,
24, 36, 38, 52, 73, 74, 82, 137,
185, 211, 239, 507, 705, C1,
C10

Name of Governing Body:
Royal Collection Trust
National

QUEEN'S HOUSE

Romney Road
Greenwich
London SE10 9NF
☎ 0181-858 4422

Queen's House

☎ 0181-293 9618 (recorded information)

This royal palace, designed by Inigo Jones for King Charles I's wife, was the first classical house to be built in England. A number of the rooms are still sumptuously decorated in silks and brocades as they were when Queen Henrietta Maria lived here. The Great Hall on the ground floor holds the National Maritime Museum's collection of paintings of seafaring and the sea.

10.00–17.00 Mon–Sat; 12.00–17.00 Sun. Closed 24–26 Dec.
£+++ Concessions (includes entry to the Old Royal Observatory and the National Maritime Museum)
A ▯ ✗
🚢 from Westminster, Charing Cross & Tower piers
⇌ Maze Hill
🚇 Island Gardens
🚌 177, 180, 188, 199, 286

Name of Governing Body:
Trustees of the National Maritime Museum
National

RAGGED SCHOOL MUSEUM

46–48 Copperfield Road
Bow
London E3 4RR
☎ 0181-980 6405

These late Victorian canal-side warehouses were converted for use as a Ragged School by Dr Barnardo. Visitors can now experience for themselves how Victorian children were taught, in a reconstructed classroom of the period. There are also displays on local history, industry and life in the East End.

Ragged School Museum

10.00–17.00 Wed & Thurs, 14.00–17.00 first Sun of each month.
£ Free S ▯
⊖ Mile End
🚌 25, 277, D5, D6, D7,

Name of Governing Body:
Ragged School Museum Trust
Independent

RANGER'S HOUSE

Chesterfield Walk
Blackheath
London SE10 8QX
☎ 0181-853 0035

This early 18th-century red-brick villa houses the Suffolk Collection of portraits, which includes major works by William Larkin, Lely and Kneller; the Dolmetsch Collection of musical instruments on loan from the Horniman Museum and the Architectural Study Collection of domestic architectural features from 17th- to 19th-century London homes.

1 Oct–31 Mar, 10.00–16.00 Wed–Sun. 1 Apr–30 Sept,

Ranger's House

10.00–13.00 & 14.00–18.00 Daily.
Closed 24 & 25 Dec & 1 Jan.
£+ Concessions A 🅿
⊖ New Cross (then bus)
≋ Blackheath, Greenwich
🚌 53, X53

Name of Governing Body:
English Heritage
Nationally funded

Riesco Collection of Chinese Ceramics

See Croydon Clocktower .

Royal Academy of Arts

Burlington House
London W1V ODS
☎ 0171-439 7438

The Academy has a programme
of major art exhibitions of
international repute made up of
loans from other galleries. Every
year since 1769 it has also
mounted its famous Summer
Exhibition of works selected from
a vast number of entries
submitted by both professional
and amateur artists. The
permanent collection is primarily

made up of works of art by Royal
Academicians.

10.00–18.00 Daily.
£+++ Concessions W E G
✗
⊖ Green Park, Piccadilly Circus
🚌 8, 9, 14, 19, 22, 38

Name of Governing Body:
**President and Council of the
Royal Academy of Arts**
Independent

Royal Air Force Museum

Grahame Park Way
Hendon
London NW9 5LL
☎ 0181-205 2266

Tells the fascinating history of
flight, including the aeroplanes
and the people who made it
possible. The museum has one of
the world's greatest collections of
historic aircraft, including the
legendary Spitfire, Hurricane,
Vulcan, Lancaster, Gladiator and
Sopwith Camel. Visitors can also
try their hand at flying a Tornado
in the exciting flight simulator.

Royal Academy of Arts

10.00–18.00 Daily.
£+++ Concessions W G ☕
✗ 🅿
⊖ Colindale
≋ Mill Hill Broadway
(Thameslink)
🚌 32, 204, 292, 302

Name of Governing Body:
Trustees of the RAF Museum
National

Royal Armouries

HM Tower of London
London EC3N 4AB
☎ 0171-480 6358

The age of chivalry captured in a
collection of tournament armour
and lances, together with a
variety of hunting weapons from
the crossbow to the pistol. The
collection includes suits of armour
worn by Henry VIII and Charles I.

Mar–Oct, 09.00–18.00 Mon–Sat,
10.00–18.00 Sun. Nov–Feb,
09.00–17.00 Mon–Sat,
10.00–17.00 Sun.
£+++ Concessions (admission to
the Tower of London) X S ☕
✗
⊖ Tower Hill
≋ London Bridge, Fenchurch St
🚌 15, 25, 42, 78, 100, D1, D9,
D11, X15

Name of Governing Body:
**Board of Trustees of the
Armouries**
National

Royal Ballet School Archive

White Lodge
Richmond Park
Surrey TW10 5HR
☎ 0181-748 7306

The archives hold material relating
to the history of ballet and ballet

dancers, together with the Royal Ballet's collection of 19th-century lithographs.

Open to researchers by written appointment.
£ Varies
⇄ Mortlake, then bus
🚌 72, 74, 85, 170, 265, 718, K6

Name of Governing Body:
Governors of the Royal Ballet School
Independent

will phone back

ROYAL COLLEGE OF MUSIC – DEPARTMENT OF PORTRAITS & PERFORMANCE HISTORY

Prince Consort Road
London SW7 2BS
☎ 0171-589 3643

A uniquely comprehensive collection of portraits of musicians, comprising some 280 original portraits and many thousands of prints and photographs. The college also holds an archive of letters from composers such as Brahms, Dvorak and Verdi, and the largest collection of concert programmes in Great Britain.

10.00–17.00 Mon–Fri by appointment.
£ Free   S   G
⊖ South Kensington
🚌 9, 9A, 10, 49, 52

Name of Governing Body:
Royal College of Music
Independent

ROYAL COLLEGE OF MUSIC – MUSEUM OF INSTRUMENTS

Prince Consort Road
London SW7 2BS
☎ 0171-589 4346

An important collection of nearly 600 keyboard, stringed and wind instruments from the 15th century to the present day, including the Tagore, Donaldson, Hipkins, Ridley and Hartley collections. The instruments are mostly European, but there are some Asian and African examples.

Term time: 14.00–16.30 Wed. Parties & special visits by appointment. Closed Jan.
£+ Concessions   S   G
⊖ South Kensington
🚌 9, 9A, 10, 49, 52, C1

Name of Governing Body:
Royal College of Music
Independent

Open by appointment
£ Free   A
⊖ Baker St
⇄ Marylebone
🚌 13, 82, 113, 274

Name of Governing Body:
Royal College of Obstetricians & Gynaecologists
Independent

Royal Armouries

ROYAL COLLEGE OF OBSTETRICIANS & GYNAECOLOGISTS

27 Sussex Place
Regent's Park
London NW1 4RG
☎ 0171 262 5425 ext 213

A collection of obstetrical and gynaecological instruments dating from the 16th century and including the Chamberlen forceps.

Royal College of Music –
Museum of Instruments

call ex 315
on Monday

ROYAL COLLEGE OF PHYSICIANS

11 St Andrew's Place
Regent's Park
London NW1 4LE
☎ 0171-935 1174 ext 374

A collection of around 350 paintings, busts, medals and miniatures of past Fellows and other notable scientific and medical personalities, from the 16th to the 20th centuries. They include works by Lely and Reynolds.

10.00–17.00 Mon–Fri.
£ Free 🅿
⊖ Regent's Park, Great Portland St
⇌ Euston
🚌 18, 27, 30, 135, C2

Name of Governing Body:
Royal College of Physicians
Independent

ROYAL FUSILIERS MUSEUM

HM Tower of London
London EC3N 4AB
☎ 0171-480 6082
☎ 0171-488 5612

Artefacts and narratives illustrating the history of the Royal Fusiliers from their foundation in 1685 to the present day.

Nov-Feb, 09.30–17.00 Mon–Sat. Mar–Oct, 09.30–18.00 Mon–Sat, 10.00–18.00 Sun.
£+++ Concessions (for Tower), additional £+ for Fusiliers Museum
⊖ Tower Hill
⇌ Fenchurch St
🚌 15, 25, 42, 78, 100, D1, D9, D11

Name of Governing Body:
The Trustees of the Royal Fusiliers Museum
Independent

ROYAL HOSPITAL CHELSEA

Royal Hospital Road
Chelsea
London SW3 4SL
☎ 0171-730 0161 ext 203

The Royal Hospital was designed by Sir Christopher Wren and built in 1682 as a retirement home for veterans of the regular army. It is still used by Chelsea Pensioners today, and it houses a small collection of objects relating to the life and history of the hospital and a collection of medals worn by pensioners.

10.00–12.00 & 14.00–16.00 Mon–Sat. Also Apr-Sept, 14.00–16.00 Sun.
£ Free A
⊖ Sloane Sq
⇌ Victoria
🚌 11, 19, 22, 137, 211, 239

Name of Governing Body:
Commissioners of the Royal Hospital
Independent

ROYAL INSTITUTE OF BRITISH ARCHITECTS

(British Architectural Library Drawings Collection & RIBA Heinz Gallery)
21 Portman Square
London W1H 9HF
☎ 0171-580 5533

Major collection of drawings and items relating to the history and practice of architecture from 1500 to the present day. Temporary exhibitions are held in the RIBA Heinz Gallery.

*Royal College of Music –
Department of Portaits and
Performance History (p 49)*

Drawings Collection: by
appointment only.
£+++ Concessions
RIBA Heinz Gallery (during
exhibitions) 11.00–17.00 Mon–Fri,
10.00–13.00 Sat.
£ Free   A   G
⊖ Marble Arch, Baker St
🚌 2, 13, 30, 74, 82, 113, 139,
159, 274

Name of Governing Body:
**Royal Institute of British
Architects**
Independent

No answer

ROYAL LONDON HOSPITAL MUSEUM AND ARCHIVES CENTRE

St Augustine with St Philip's
Church
Newark Street
London E1 2AA
☎ 0171-377 7000 ext 3364

The story of the hospital from its
foundation in 1740. Displays look
at the hospital's contribution to
the health of millions of
Londoners and at the work of
famous figures such as Dr
Barnardo and Edith Cavell.
Modern developments such as
London's first Helicopter
Emergency Service are the subject
of temporary displays.
10.00–16.30 Mon–Fri. Closed
Public Hols.
£ Free   X   G   ☕   ✗
⊖ Whitechapel
🚇 Bethnal Green
🚌 25, 253

Name of Governing Body:
The Royal Hospitals NHS Trust
Independent

ROYAL MILITARY SCHOOL OF MUSIC

Kneller Hall
Kneller Road
Twickenham
Middlesex TW2 7DU
☎ 0181-898 5533

This huge Jacobean-style mansion
houses the Royal Military School
of Music and a small museum
with displays of bandsmen's
uniforms, musical militaria and
wind and stringed instruments
played in military bands.

Open by appointment.
£ Free   ☕

🚇 Twickenham, Whitton
🚌 281, R62

Name of Governing Body:
**Board of Trustees of the Royal
Military School of Music**
Independent

ROYAL OPERA HOUSE ARCHIVES

Royal Opera House
Floral Street
Covent Garden
London WC2E 9DD
☎ 0171-240 1200 ext 353

This extensive collection
documents the history of the

Royal Opera House's three companies, the Royal Ballet, the Birmingham Royal Ballet and the Royal Opera. Material includes photographs, prints, plans and playbills.

10.30–13.00 & 14.30–17.30 Mon, Tues, Thurs & Fri, by appointment to researchers only. Foyer displays open to theatre-goers.
£ Free/research fee
⊖ Covent Garden
⇌ Charing Cross
🚌 1, 6, 9, 11, 13, 15, 23, 68, 77A, 91, 168, 171, 176, 188, 501, 505, 521, X15, X68

Name of Governing Body:
Royal Opera House Company
Independent

0267 3288299

SAATCHI COLLECTION

98a Boundary Road
London NW8 0RH
☎ 0171-624 8299

This major private collection of contemporary art, started in 1970, contains sculpture and paintings primarily by American and British artists. Works can be seen on display in the vast and light-filled Saatchi Gallery in a changing series of exhibitions.

12.00–18.00 Thurs–Sun.
£++ (Thurs free) S G
⊖ St John's Wood, Swiss Cottage
⇌ South Hampstead
🚌 31, 139

Name of Governing Body:
Privately owned *£5*
Independent *£3/conc*
call Philli on monday.

ST BARTHOLOMEW'S HOSPITAL ANAESTHETICS MUSEUM

West Smithfield
London EC1A 7BE
☎ 0171-601 8888 ext 7518

The hospital houses a large collection for the study and teaching of the evolution of anaesthetics.

Open to researchers by appointment.
£ Free
⊖ Barbican, St Paul's
⇌ Moorgate
🚌 4, 8, 22B, 25, 56, 153, 172, 279, 501

Name of Governing Body:
Privately administered
Independent

ST BARTHOLOMEW'S HOSPITAL ARCHIVES

West Smithfield
London EC1A 7BE
☎ 0171-601 8152

The archives contain paintings, silverware and furniture together with archaeological finds from the hospital site and documents relating to the history of St Bartholomew's.

Open to researchers by appointment.
£ Free ♟ ✗
⊖ St Paul's, Barbican
⇌ Moorgate
🚌 4, 8, 22B, 25, 56, 153, 172, 279, 501

Name of Governing Body:
The Royal Hospitals NHS Trust
Independent

ST BERNARD'S HOSPITAL MUSEUM

Uxbridge Road
Southall
Middlesex UB1 3EU
☎ 0181-967 5183
☎ 0181-574 2444

The museum houses a collection of archival material dating back to

the founding of the hospital in 1831, and relating to the treatment of psychiatric patients. There are also a small number of related artefacts such as leather restraints.

09.00–17.00 Mon–Fri by appointment. Children under 16 yrs are only allowed in if accompanied by an adult.
£+ 🅿
⊖ Ealing Broadway, Ealing Common
⇌ Hanwell, Southall, Ealing Braodway
🚌 83, 92, 195, 207, 282, 607

Name of Governing Body:
West London Healthcare NHS Trust
Independent

ST BRIDE'S CRYPT EXHIBITION

St Bride's Church
Fleet Street
London EC4Y 8AU
☎ 0171-353 1301

The current church, the eighth to occupy the site, was designed by Sir Christopher Wren and rebuilt after bomb damage during World War II. The museum in the crypt tells the history of the seven previous churches, dating from the 6th century. There are also displays on the development of printing and the newspaper industry in Fleet Street.

09.00–17.00 Daily.
£ Free
⊖ Blackfriars
⇌ Blackfriars, City Thameslink
🚌 4, 11, 15, 23, 26, 45, 63, 76, 172, X15

Name of Governing Body:
Rector and Churchwardens
Independent

SALVATION ARMY INTERNATIONAL HERITAGE CENTRE

117–121 Judd Street
King's Cross
London WC1H 9NN
☎ 0171-387 1656 ext 244/256

Salvation Army history from 1865 to the present day. Amongst the exhibits are photographs, documents and objects from the everyday life of William Booth and his followers. An audio tour guide is available.

09.30–15.30 Mon–Fri,
09.30–12.30 Sat.
£ Free X G Ⓥ
⊖ King's Cross, Euston
⇌ King's Cross St Pancras,
🚌 10, 17, 18, 30, 45, 46, 63, 73, 91, 214, 259, C12

Name of Governing Body:
The Salvation Army
Independent

SCIENCE MUSEUM

Exhibition Road
South Kensington
London SW7 2DD
☎ 0171-938 8000/8008/8080

Outstanding collections form an unparalleled record of mankind's greatest inventions and achievements. There are nearly a thousand working exhibits with a chance to try out your own experiments in 'Launch Pad', the interactive gallery, or test your skill at flying a model jump jet in 'Flight Lab'. Includes the Wellcome Museum of the History of Medicine.

10.00–18.00 Daily.
£+++ Concessions W G 🍽 X

Science Museum

⊖ South Kensington
🚌 9, 10, 14, 45, 49, 52, 70, 74, C1

Name of Governing Body:
Trustees of the Science Museum
National

SHAKESPEARE'S GLOBE EXHIBITION

Bear Gardens
Bankside
Liberty of the Clink
London SE1 9EB
☎ 0171-928 6406

An exhibition tracing the vivid history of the Elizabethan and Jacobean theatre and Elizabethan Bankside – London's first entertainment district. Displays also show how Shakespeare's Globe is being rebuilt on the same site using authentic Elizabethan building materials and techniques.

10.00–17.00 Mon–Sat,
14.00–17.30 Sun.
£++ Concessions   S   Ⓥ

⊖ Mansion House, Cannon St, London Bridge
≋ London Bridge
🚌 21, 35, 40, 133, 344, D1, D11, P3, P11

Name of Governing Body:
Shakespeare Globe Trust
Independent

SILVER STUDIO COLLECTION

Middlesex University
Bounds Green Road
London N11 2NQ
☎ 0181-368 1299 ext 7339

A wonderful collection of wallpaper and textile designs produced by the Silver Studio, one of the leading independent design studios from the 1880s until the 1950s.

10.00–16.00 Mon–Fri,
appointments appreciated.
£ Free   Ⓥ   ☕
⊖ Bounds Green
≋ Bowes Park, New Southgate
🚌 221, 232

Silver Studio Collection

Name of Governing Body:
Middlesex University
University

SIR JOHN SOANE'S MUSEUM

13 Lincoln's Inn Fields
London WC2A 3BP
☎ 0171-405 2107
☎ 0171-430 0175 (information)

Built by Sir John Soane RA in 1812–1813 as his private residence, the museum is a warren of fantastically titled rooms such as the Sepulchral Chamber and the Monk's Parlour. The building is crammed with Soane's accumulated collection of treasures – Greek, Roman and Egyptian antiquities and 18th- and 19th-century furniture, works of art and architectural drawings.

10.00–17.00 Tues–Sat, also 18.00–21.00 first Tues of each month.Library/archives by appointment.
£ Free   S
⊖ Holborn
🚌 1, 8, 19, 22B, 25, 38, 55, 68, 91, 98, 168, 171, 188, 501, 505, 521

Name of Governing Body:
Trustees of Sir John Soane's Museum
National

SOSEKI MUSEUM IN LONDON

80b The Chase
London SW4
☎ 0171-720 8718

Museum devoted to the distinguished Japanese novelist Soseki Natsume, who lived in this house briefly at the beginning of the century.

Feb–Sep, 10.00–12.00 & 14.00–17.00 Wed & Sat,

14.00–17.00 Sun. Oct-Jan, by appointment only.
£+ Concessions S **P**
⊖ Clapham Common
⇌ Wandsworth Road
🚌 45A, 60, 77, 77A, 88, 137, 137A

Name of Governing Body:
Trustees of the Soseki Natsume Museum
Independent

SOUTH LONDON GALLERY

65 Peckham Road
London SE5 8UH
☎ 0171-703 6120

This purpose-built gallery, opened in 1891, houses a series of temporary exhibitions of contemporary art and of works from its permanent collections of British art (c.1700 onwards) and 20th-century original prints.

10.00–18.00 Tues, Wed & Fri. 10.00–19.00 Thurs, 14.00–18.00 Sat & Sun. Closed Mon & Bank Hols.
£ Free S G **P**
⊖ Elephant & Castle; Oval, then bus
⇌ Peckham Rye
🚌 12, 36, 45A, 171

Name of Governing Body:
London Borough of Southwark
Local Authority

SOUTHALL RAILWAY CENTRE

(entrance via footbridge linking Merrick Road & Park Avenue)
Southall
Middlesex UB2 4PL
☎ 0181-574 1529
☎ 0181-574 8100 (events information)

This railway museum, housed in a former steam and diesel depot, has a large collection of rolling stock and a number of engines still in working condition. There is an exciting programme of special events, including an opportunity to learn to drive a steam engine.

11.00–18.00 Sat & Sun.
£+ Concessions (prices for events vary) 🍴 **P**
⇌ Southall
🚌 105, 120, 195, E5, H32

Name of Governing Body:
GWR Preservation Group Ltd
Independent

CLOSED DOWN. SPRINGFIELD HOSPITAL MUSEUM

61 Glenburnie Road
London SW17 7DJ
☎ 0181-672 9911

This small, but intriguing, museum houses a collection of documents and artefacts relating to the history of Springfield psychiatric hospital.

Open by appointment.
£ Free **P**
⊖ Tooting Bec
🚌 115, 155, 219, 249, 319, 355, G2

Name of Governing Body:
Springfield Hospital
Independent phone back tues, wed, thurs 2-4

STEPHENS COLLECTION

Avenue House
East End Road
Finchley
London N3 3QE
☎ 0181-346 7812 (information)
☎ 0181-346 6337

Avenue House was bought in 1874 by Henry 'Inky' Stephens, who then added a laboratory where he carried out his experiments with writing fluids. The house now contains displays on the development of writing instruments through the ages, the life of Henry Stephens and the history of Avenue House and the Stephens Ink Company.

14.00–16.30 Tues–Thurs.
£ Free 🍴 **P**
⊖ Finchley Central
⇌ Oakleigh Park
🚌 13, 82, 143, 260, 326

Name of Governing Body:
The Finchley Society
Independent

SUTTON HOUSE

2 & 4 Homerton High Street
Hackney
London E9 6JQ
☎ 0181-986 2264

The oldest house in east London, built in 1535, contains 16th-century panelling and decorated fireplaces, 17th-century wall

Sutton House

paintings, and a Tudor well. There is also a permanent historic exhibition and a contemporary art gallery.

11.30–17.00 Wed & Sun. Feb–Nov, also 11.30–17.00 Bank Hol Mons. Closed Good Friday. Art gallery, shop and cafe also open Thurs–Sat.
£+ Concessions W ● ✗
⇌ Hackney Central, Homerton
🚌 22B, 30, 38, 55, 236, 276, S2, W15

Name of Governing Body:
National Trust
Independent

SYON HOUSE

Syon Park
Brentford
Middlesex TW8 8JF
☎ 0181-560 0881

This magnificent Tudor house, the property of the Dukes of Northumberland, was Lady Jane Grey's home for the nine days after she accepted the crown of England and before she was taken to the Tower and later executed. Part of the interior was remodelled in the 17th century by Robert Adam and the gardens were laid out by Capability Brown at the same time. The house contains an important collection of paintings including works by Gainsborough, Reynolds, Van Dyck and Lely.

Apr–end Sept, 11.00–17.00 weekends & Bank Hols, last admission 16.15. Gardens open daily 10.00–18.00 or until dusk.
£+++ Concessions X E ●
✗
⇌ Syon Lane, Brentford
🚌 116, 117, 237, 267

Name of Governing Body:
Privately owned
Independent

YR 2000 1,204,147

TATE GALLERY

Millbank
London SW1P 4RG
☎ 0171-887 8000
☎ 0171-887 8008 (recorded information)

The Tate Gallery houses two great collections, one of British art from the 16th century to the present day and the other of international 20th-century painting and sculpture. The displays are rehung every year so that works that have been kept in storage can be viewed. The Tate also mounts a programme of major exhibitions including art loaned from galleries worldwide. The Clore Gallery, attached to the main building of

the Tate, shows paintings and watercolours by Turner.

10.00–17.50 Mon–Sat,
14.00–17.50 Sun.
£ Free W E G Ⓥ ● ✗
⊖ Pimlico
⇌ Vauxhall
🚌 2, 36, 77A, 88, 185, C10

Name of Governing Body:
The Trustees of the Tate Gallery
National

With own bmk
202,800
THEATRE MUSEUM

(entrance on Russell Street)
1e Tavistock Street
Covent Garden
London WC2E 7PA
☎ 0171-836 7891 020 794
347
00

TATE MODERN 3,831,651 → £5 – 8.50 for special exhibs

Britain's theatrical and performing arts heritage is on display in this captivating museum – from Shakespeare's First Folio to Mick Jagger's jump suit. The story of the performing arts is told with the help of costumes, prints and drawings, posters, puppets, props and a vast collection of memorabilia.

11.00–19.00 Tues–Sun.
£++ Concessions   W   G
⊖ Covent Garden
≷ Charing Cross
🚌 1, 6, 9, 11, 13, 15, 23, 68, 77A, 91, 168, 171, 176, 188, 501, 505, 521, X68

Name of Governing Body:
Trustees of the Victoria & Albert Museum
National

THOMAS CORAM FOUNDATION FOR CHILDREN

40 Brunswick Square
London WC1N 1AZ
☎ 0171-270 2424
NUMBER CHANGED
Built on the site of the original Foundling Hospital, the building now contains an important collection of 18th-century British paintings, and musical scores by Handel and others connected with the foundation.

Temporarily closed to casual visitors. Tours by arrangement.
£+ Concessions   A   G
⊖ Russell Sq
≷ King's Cross, St Pancras
🚌 17, 45, 46, 68, 91, 168, 188

Name of Governing Body:
Thomas Coram Foundation for Children
Independent

TOWER BRIDGE EXHIBITION

Tower Bridge
London SE1 2UP
☎ 0171-403 3761

Tower Bridge Exhibition

Situated inside the twin towers of the bridge, the exhibition gives an insight into the history, design and operation of this unique structure. Visitors can also enjoy panoramic views over London from the high-level walkways and see the original Victorian engines.

Apr–Oct, 10.00–17.15 Daily.
Nov–Mar, 09.30–16.30 Daily.
Closed 1 Jan, 24–26 Dec & Good Friday.
£+++ Concessions   X   G   Ⓥ
⊖ Tower Hill, London Bridge
⚓ to Tower Pier
🚋 Tower Gateway
≷ London Bridge, Fenchurch St
🚌 15, 42, 78, 100, D1, P11

Name of Governing Body:
Corporation of London
Local Authority

TOWER HILL PAGEANT

Tower Hill
London EC3N 4EE
☎ 0171-709 0081

Ride through 2, 000 years of history, seeing, hearing and smelling the past in London's first dark-ride museum. Displays include over 1, 000 Roman and medieval finds.

09.30–17.30 Daily. Closes 16.30 in winter.
£+++ Concessions   X   Ⓥ   ☕
✕
⊖ Tower Hill
≷ Fenchurch St, London Bridge
🚌 15, 25, 42, 78, 100, D1, D9, D11

Name of Governing Body:
Culverin Consortium Limited
Independent

TRADES UNION CONGRESS COLLECTION

Congress House
Great Russell Street
London WC1B 3LS
☎ 0171-636 4030

The collection includes archives and memorabilia relating to the history of the Trades Union Congress.

Open for research by appointment.
£ Free
⊖ Tottenham Court Rd
🚌 7, 8, 10, 14, 19, 22B, 24, 25, 29, 38, 55, 73, 98, 134, 176, 501, 505, 521

Name of Governing Body:
Trades Union Congress
Independent

TWININGS IN THE STRAND

216 The Strand
London WC2
☎ 0171-353 3511

This small-scale museum, ingeniously housed in the Twinings shop, has an engaging series of displays on the history of tea.

09.30–16.00 Mon–Fri (large groups not possible).

Valence House Museum

£ Free   X
⊖ Temple, Aldwych
⇌ Charing Cross
🚌 1, 4, 6, 9, 11, 13, 15, 23, 26, 68, 76, 77A, 91, 168, 171, 176, 188, 501, 505, 521, X15, X68

Name of Governing Body:
R Twining and Company Limited
Independent

UNIVERSITY COLLEGE ART COLLECTION

Strang Print Room
University College
Gower Street
London WC1E 6BT   NOT RECOG
☎ 0171-387 7050 ext 2540

An important collection of fine art including European prints, drawings and paintings, Japanese prints, and sculptures by Flaxman. Works are displayed in the Flaxman Gallery and the Strang Print Room.

Term time, 13.00–14.30 Mon–Fri.
£ Free   X   G

⊖ Warren St, Euston, Euston Sq, Goodge St
⇌ Euston
🚌 10, 24, 29, 73, 134

Name of Governing Body:
University College Art Collections Committee
University

UNIVERSITY COLLEGE DEPARTMENT OF GEOLOGICAL SCIENCES COLLECTION

Department of Geological Sciences
University College
Gower Street
London WC1E 6BT
☎ 0171-387 7050

Teaching and research collection of geological specimens including a print and photograph collection.

Collections open by appointment. Rock Room (Room 4, South Wing) also open 12.30–14.00 Wed without appointment.
£ Free   V   🍴   X
⊖ Euston Sq, Goodge St, Warren St, Euston
⇌ Euston, King's Cross
🚌 10, 24, 29, 30, 73, 134

Name of Governing Body:
University College London
University

UPMINSTER TITHE BARN

Hall Lane
Upminster
Essex RM14 1AU
☎ 01708-447535

This large 15th-century thatched barn contains the Hornchurch & District Historical Society's collections of agricultural implements and domestic items relating to the local area.

Apr–Oct, 14.00–18.00 1st weekend in each month.
£ Free   X   G   🅿
⊖ Upminster
⇌ Upminster
🚌 248

Name of Governing Body:
Hornchurch & District Historical Society
Independent

UPMINSTER WINDMILL

St Mary's Lane
Upminster
Essex RM14 2QL
☎ 01708-772394

This smock windmill was built in 1801 and still contains all its original machinery. There are regular conducted tours led by guides who can explain the mill's workings.

Apr–Oct, 14.00–17.30 Sat & Sun on the 3rd weekend of each month.
£ Free   V
⊖ Upminster
⇌ Upminster
🚌 246, 248, 370

Name of Governing Body:
Hornchurch & District Historical Society
Independent

VALENCE HOUSE MUSEUM

Becontree Avenue
Dagenham
Essex RM8 3HT
☎ 0181-595 8404

Built in the 17th century and still partially surrounded by a medieval moat, this timber-framed manor house now contains a permanent display on the history of Barking and Dagenham as well as the 17th-century Fanshawe family portraits. There is also a period-style herb garden in the grounds.

09.30–13.00 & 14.00–16.30
Tues–Fri, 10.00–16.00 Sat.
£ Free   S   P
≥ Chadwell Heath
🚌 5, 62, 87, 128, 129, 364, 368
Name of Governing Body:
**London Borough of Barking
and Dagenham**
Local Authority

VESTRY HOUSE MUSEUM

Vestry Road
Walthamstow
London E17 9NH
☎ 0181-509 1917

Waltham Forest's local history
museum is housed in this early
18th-century workhouse. There
are permanent displays on local
domestic life, a reconstructed
Victorian parlour and a 19th-
century police cell. The Bremer
Car (1894), Britain's first motor
vehicle, was built locally and can
also be seen here.

10.00–13.00 & 14.00–17.30
Mon–Fri, 10.00–13.00 & 14.00–
17.00 Sat. Closed Bank Hols.
£ Free   S   G   P
⊖ Walthamstow Central
≥ Walthamstow Central

🚌 2, 20, 25, 34, 48, 58, 69, 97,
212, 215, 230, 257, 275, 505,
551, W11, W15

Name of Governing Body:
**London Borough of Waltham
Forest**
Local Authority

VETERINARY MUSEUM

The Royal Veterinary College
Royal College Street
London NW1 0TU
☎ 0171-468 5000

Museum with displays of items of
general veterinary historical
interest. Also the Royal Veterinary
College historical collection.

09.00–16.45 Mon–Fri, by
appointment only.
£ Free   V
⊖ King's Cross, Camden Town
≥ King's Cross
🚌 46, 214

Name of Governing Body:
The Royal Veterinary College
University

Victoria & Albert Museum

VICTORIA & ALBERT MUSEUM ○ 2079422

Cromwell Road
London SW7 2RL
☎ 0171-938 8500

The national collections of
sculpture, furniture, textiles and
dress, ceramics and glass, silver,
jewellry and metalwork drawn
from both European and
non-Western cultures. The V&A
also holds extensive collections of
prints, photographs and
paintings, including the
Constable collection. There is a
changing programme of exciting
temporary exhibitions.

10.00–17.50 Tues–Sun,
12.00–17.50 Mon.
£ Free, but donation requested
W   E   G   P   X
⊖ South Kensington,
Knightsbridge
≥ Victoria
🚌 14, 45A, 49, 70, 74, C1

Name of Governing Body:
**Trustees of the Victoria &
Albert Museum**
National

VINTAGE WIRELESS MUSEUM

23 Rosendale Road
West Dulwich
London SE21 8DS
☎ 0181-670 3667

This extraordinary collection of
around 1, 000 radios and
televisions has been built up by
enthusiast Gerald Wells. It now fills
to overflowing the Victorian house
where he was born and still lives.

Open by appointment only.
£ Free   P   P
≥ West Dulwich, Tulse Hill
🚌 3, 115, S11

Name of Governing Body:
The Vintage Wireless Museum
Independent

2 44,000 last yr everything free

WALLACE COLLECTION

Hertford House
Manchester Square
London W1M 6BN
☎ 0171-935 0687

A permanent collection of Old Master paintings, French 18th-century furniture, ceramics, goldsmiths' work, miniatures, sculpture, and European and Oriental arms and armour.

10.00–17.00 Mon–Sat,
14.00–17.00 Sun.
£ Free X G
⊖ Marble Arch, Bond St, Baker St
🚌 2, 6, 7, 8, 10, 12, 13, 15, 16A, 23, 30, 73, 74, 82, 113, 135, 137, 139, 159, 274

Name of Governing Body:
Trustees of the Wallace Collection
National

WANDLE INDUSTRIAL MUSEUM

The Vestry Hall Annexe
London Road
Mitcham
Surrey CR4 3UD
☎ 0181-648 0127

The museum tells the history of the Wandle Valley and its industrial heritage through displays of photographs, archives and social and industrial artefacts. It will be moving to new premises at Ravensbury Mill, Morden, Surrey in late 1995. Please telephone for details.
13.00–16.00 Wed, 14.00–17.00 first Sun of each month. Open to schools and groups by appointment.

£+
🚈 Mitcham
🚌 118, 127, 200, 270, 280, 355

Name of Governing Body:
Wandle Industrial Museum Trust
Independent

WANDSWORTH MUSEUM

The Courthouse
Garratt Lane
Wandsworth
London SW18
☎ 0181-871 7074

The new Wandsworth Museum will open in spring 1996 and will tell the history of the Borough.

There will be special displays on what life was like in the villages which now make up Wandsworth and the first floor will also contain a temporary exhibitions gallery.

Contact museum for details.
£ Free W G E
🚈 Wandsworth Town
🚌 23, 37, 44, 77A, 220, 270, 337

Name of Governing Body:
London Borough of Wandsworth
Local Authority

WELLCOME TRUST EXHIBITIONS

Wellcome Building
183 Euston Road
London NW1 2BE

Two 10 Gallery
210 Euston Road
London NW1 2BE
☎ 0171-611 8727 (recorded information)
☎ 0171-611 8888 (enquiries)

Wellcome Centre for Medical Science: *Science for Life*. A permanent exhibition about biomedicine featuring extensive use of the latest interactive technology and a giant reconstruction of a cell, which visitors can walk into and explore. *Two 10 Gallery*. A series of temporary exhibitions exploring the interaction between art and the medical sciences.

Wellcome Institute for the History of Medicine: *History of Medicine Gallery*. Lively programme of thematic exhibitions, based largely on the collections of the Wellcome Institute Library.

Wallace Collection

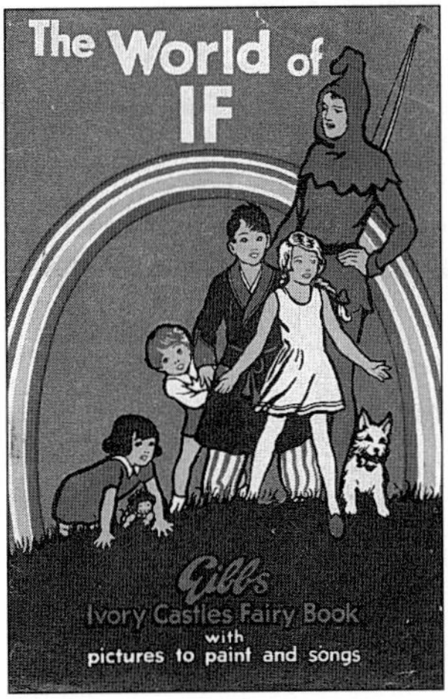

Wellcome Trust Exhibitions

9.45–17.00 Mon–Fri, 9.45–13.00 (except Two 10 Gallery) Sat.
£ Free
⊖ Euston, Euston Sq
⇌ Euston
🚌 10, 14, 18, 24, 27, 29, 30, 73, 74, 134, 135

Name of Governing Body:
The Wellcome Trust
Independent

Wesley's Chapel

(incorporating Wesley's House and the Museum of Methodism)
49 City Road
London EC1Y 1AU
☎ 0171-253 2262

Built by John Wesley in 1778 as a base for his work in London. The chapel's crypt now houses a museum tracing the history of Methodism from the 18th century to the present day. Wesley's personal belongings are housed next door in the home where he lived for 12 years, and Wesley himself is buried to the rear of the chapel.

10.00–16.00 Mon–Sat, 12.00–14.00 Sun.
£++ Concessions W G
⊖ Old St, Moorgate
⇌ Old St, Moorgate
🚌 5, 43, 55, 76, 141, 214, 243, 271, 505, X43

Name of Governing Body:
The Methodist Church
Independent

Westminster Abbey Museum

Westminster Abbey
London SW1P 3PA
☎ 0171-222 5152

A collection of wooden and wax effigies modelled from the death masks of medieval and Tudor monarchs and nobles. Some of the effigies are clothed in contemporary costume and paste jewellery; the Duchess of Richmond is even accompanied by her stuffed pet parrot.

10.30 16.00 Daily.
£++ Concessions X G ☕
⊖ Westminster, St James's Park
⇌ Victoria
🚌 3, 11, 12, 24, 53, 77A, 88, 109, 159, 211, X53

Name of Governing Body:
The Dean & Chapter of Westminster
Independent

Westminster Dragoons Museum

Cavalry House
Duke of Yorks HQ
King's Road
Chelsea
London SW3 4SC
☎ 0171-821 8560

Collection of material, dating from the late 18th century onwards, relating to the history of the regiment and including

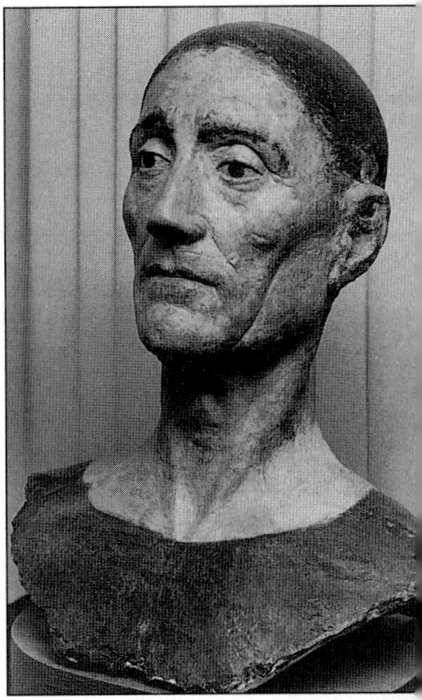

Henry VII – Westminster Abbey Museum

uniforms, weapons, paintings, prints and other archival material.

Open by appointment.
£ Free 🅿
⊖ Sloane Sq
🚌 11, 19, 22, 137, 137A, 211, 249, 319, C1

Name of Governing Body:
Berkshire & Westminster Dragoons Museum Trust
Independent

Whitehall, Cheam

1 Malden Road
Cheam
Surrey SM3 8QD
☎ 0181-643 1236
☎ 0181-770 4781

This timber-framed house, built in about 1500, features permanent displays on medieval Cheam pottery, Nonsuch Palace and Cheam School, as well as a changing exhibition programme.

Apr–Sept, 14.00–17.30 Tues–Fri & Sun, 10.00–17.30 Sat. Oct–Mar, 14.00–17.30 Wed, Thurs, Sun, 10.00–17.30 Sat. Open all Bank Hol Mons 14.00–17.30. Closed 24 Dec–2 Jan.
£+ Concessions X G 🍵
⊖ Morden
⇌ Cheam
🚌 151, 213, 408, 726

Name of Governing Body:
London Borough of Sutton
Local Authority

WILKINSON SWORD MUSEUM

19–21 Brunel Road
Acton
London W3 7UH
☎ 0181-749 1061
Collection of swords and guns.

Open by appointment.
£ Free 🅿
⊖ East Acton
🚌 7, 70, 72, 283

Name of Governing Body:
Wilkinson Sword Ltd
Independent

WILLIAM MORRIS GALLERY

Lloyd Park
Forest Road
London E17 4PP
☎ 0181-527 3782

William Morris's childhood home provides a delightful setting in which to discover the achievements and influence of this remarkable man. The collection includes wallpaper, tapestries, furniture and ceramics designed by Morris and his associates. You can also see the Frank Brangwyn gift of Pre-Raphaelite paintings and drawings.

10.00–13.00 & 14.00–17.00 Tues–Sat & first Sun of each month.
£ Free A G 🅿
⊖ Walthamstow Central
⇌ Walthamstow Central
🚌 39, 97, 97A, 123, 215, 275

Name of Governing Body:
London Borough of Waltham Forest
Local Authority

William Morris Gallery

WILLIAM MORRIS SOCIETY

Kelmscott House
26 Upper Mall
Hammersmith
London W6 9TA
☎ 0181-741 3735

This elegant riverside house was William Morris's home from 1878 until his death in 1896. It now contains displays of his wallpaper and fabric designs together with some of the 52 books printed by the Kelmscott Press, a private printing establishment which was set up by Morris and housed nearby.

14.00–17.00 Thurs & Sat.
£ Free S G
⊖ Ravenscourt Park
🚌 27, 237, 266, 267, 290, 391, 415, 702, E3, H91

Name of Governing Body:
William Morris Society
Independent

Wimbledon Lawn Tennis Museum

WIMBLEDON LAWN TENNIS MUSEUM

The All England Club
Church Road
London SW19 5AE
☎ 0181-946 6131

The story of how this sport, once the rage on the lawns of Victorian England, has grown to become an international, multi-million dollar business. The collection includes some fascinating examples of tennis fashions and accessories.

10.30–17.00 Tues–Sat, 14.00–17.00 Sun. Closed Mon, Bank Hols & Fri, Sat & Sun prior to the championships. Also closed middle Sun of the championships.
£++ Concessions W G ✗
⊖ Southfields, Wimbledon Park
⇌ Wimbledon
🚌 39, 93, 156

Name of Governing Body:
The All England Lawn Tennis Ground Ltd
Independent

WIMBLEDON SOCIETY MUSEUM

26 Lingfield Road
Wimbledon
London SW19 4QD
☎ 0181-946 9398

Displays of material relating to Wimbledon and its history, including natural history specimens, archaeology, manuscripts and a collection of old photographs, prints and watercolours of the area.

14.30–17.00 Sat, otherwise by appointment.
£ Free   S
⊖ Wimbledon
⇌ Wimbledon
🚌 93, 200

Name of Governing Body:
The Wimbledon Society
Independent

WIMBLEDON WINDMILL MUSEUM

Windmill Road
Wimbledon Common
London SW19 5NR
☎ 0181-947 2825

This windmill was built in 1817 on Wimbledon Common and was operated for the next 50 years. It now houses a museum of the history of windmilling told in pictures and through the actual tools and machinery used. Many of the exhibits can be handled and there are a number of working models to show how wind power has been harnessed.

Easter–end Oct, 14.00–17.00 Sat, Sun & Public Hols. Nov–Mar, open for group visits & schools.
£+ Concessions S G 🍴 🅿
⊖ Wimbledon, Putney
⇌ Wimbledon, Putney
🚌 85, 93, 264, 740

Name of Governing Body:
Wimbledon Windmill Museum Trust
Independent

BENJAMIN FRANKLIN HOUSE

Friends of Benjamin Franklin
59 Great Ormond Street
London WC1N 3HZ
☎ 0171-430 2384

Planned restoration of 36 Craven Street, the only surviving home of Benjamin Franklin, as a museum, library and conference centre.

Name of Governing Body:
Friends of Benjamin Franklin House
Independent

CINEMA MUSEUM

The Old Fire Station
46 Renfrew Road
Kennington
London SE11 4NA
☎ 0171-820 9992

History of cinemas from 1898 to the present day. In storage, but can be viewed by appointment.

Name of Governing Body:
Board of Directors of the Cinema Museum
Independent

CROSSNESS ENGINES TRUST

c/o The Secretary
8 Yorkland Avenue
Welling
Kent DA16 2LF
☎ 0181-303 6723

Four Victorian pumping engines built by James Watt & Co. 1860s. Occasional open days and two visitor days a month (booking required), telephone for details.

Name of Governing Body:
Crossness Engines Trust
Independent

CROYDON AIRPORT SOCIETY

Sutton Libraries & Heritage Department
Head Office
Central Library
St Nicholas Way
Surrey SM1 1EA
Enquiries c/o ☎ 0181-770 4750

Collection of photographs, ephemera and objects relating to Croydon Airport.

Name of Governing Body:
Croydon Airport Society
Independent

GIRL GUIDES MUSEUM

Girl Guides Association
17–19 Buckingham Palace Road
London SW1W OPT
☎ 0171-834 6242

Film, photographs, costume and personalia relating to the International Girl Guide movement. Due to open early in 1996.

Name of Governing Body:
The Girl Guides Association
Independent

HANDEL HOUSE

The Handel House Trust Ltd
12 Lyndhurst Rd
London NW3 5NL
☎ 0171-435 2482
temporarily out of order
Museum based at 25 Brook Street, Mayfair, where the composer lived for 36 years and composed the Messiah. Will open in mid 1997 and offer recreations of the rooms in which Handel lived and worked as well as exhibition, concert, lecture and research facilities.

Name of Governing Body:
Handel House Association Ltd
Independent

HOUSE MILL MUSEUM PROJECT

c/o 84 Richmond Road
London SW10 0PD
☎ 0181-947 8702

Restoration of 1776 House Mill, with visitor centre.

Name of Governing Body:
River Lea Tidal Mill Trust
Independent

MARKFIELD BEAM ENGINE AND MUSEUM

Markfield Road
South Tottenham
London N15 4RB
☎ 0181-800 7061

Original compound beam pumping engine, built in 1886 and restored to working order. Telephone for details of opening days.

Name of Governing Body:
Markfield Beam Engine and Museum
Independent

METROPOLITAN POLICE MUSEUM

c/o Room 1328A
New Scotland Yard
London SW1H OBG
☎ 0181-305 2824

Museum is currently seeking a new site, whilst the branches, the Mounted Police Museum and the Thames River Police Museum are open by appointment.

Name of Governing Body:
Metropolitan Police Museum Trust
Independent

(handwritten) will call back

MILLWALL FC MUSEUM

Millwall FC
Zampa Road
London SE16 3LN
☎ 0171-232 1222
Museum on the history of Millwall
Football Club with reference to
the Isle of Dogs, east London and
New Cross, Bermondsey and
south-east London. Opening
planned for autumn 1995.

MUSEUM IN DOCKLANDS

c/o Unit C14
Poplar Business Park
10 Preston's Road
London E14 9RL
☎ 0171-515 1162

The history of London's river, port,
commerce and industry, opening
in summer 1997. A loan and
resource service is currently
available to schools. The 'Museum
on the Move' will transport
temporary displays around the
local area.

Name of Governing Body:
**Steering Committee for the
Museum of the Port of London
and Docklands**
Independent

(handwritten) will call back maybe

MUSEUM OF SOHO

St Anne's Tower
55 Dean Street
London W1V 5HH
☎ 0171-439 4303

Permanent collection of local
history, archive material and
books with temporary displays. In
storage, but can be viewed by
appointment.

Name of Governing Body:
Museum of Soho Ltd
Independent

MUSEUM OF WOMEN'S ART

Second Floor
North Suite
55–63 Goswell Road
London EC1V 7EN
☎ 0171-251 4881

Project to establish a permanent
exhibition of national and
international significance for the
exhibition, research and study of
women's art.

Name of Governing Body:
**Board of Trustees of Museum
of Women's Art**
Independent

OUTSIDER ARCHIVE/COLLECTION

c/o 213 South Lambeth Road
London SW8 1XR
☎ 0171-735 2192
(handwritten) fax number
Plans to open a museum to house
an international collection of
works by artists working outside
the cultural tradition.

Name of Governing Body:
Victor Musgrave Outsider Trust
Independent

REDBRIDGE MUSEUM

Central Library
Clements Road
Ilford IG1 1EA
☎ 0181-478 7145

Items relating to the local history
of Redbridge and its predecessor
authorities. A permanent site is
planned, meanwhile some items
can be seen on display in the
central library.

Name of Governing Body:
London Borough of Redbridge
Local Authority

ST. MARK'S CHURCH (SILVERTOWN E16)

c/o Newham Museum Service
North Woolwich Old Station
Museum
Pier Road
North Woolwich
London E16 2JJ
☎ 0181-474 7244

St Mark's Church has been
restored to house a museum
about the surrounding Victorian
dockland suburbs.

Name of Governing Body:
**Governors of the Passmore
Edwards Museum**
Local Authority

TYPE MUSEUM

16 Groveway
London SW9 0AR
☎ 0171-735 7791

Collection of over 8,000 items
relating to printing, including
patterns, punches and matrixes
and machinery.

Name of Governing Body:
Merrion Monotype Trust
Independent

WHITEWEBBS MUSEUM OF TRANSPORT AND INDUSTRY

Whitewebbs Road
Enfield
Middlesex EN2 9HW
☎ 0181-367 1898

Project to restore and convert the
former new river pump house
(built 1898) into a transport
museum to house a collection of
early vehicles. Telephone for
details of open days.

Name of Governing Body:
**The Enfield and District
Veteran Vehicle Trust**
Independent

(handwritten) it seemed they had about 20 answer messages, so not sure if still active

THE COMPLETE ONE-STOP PUBLISHING SERVICE

BOOK PRODUCTION CONSULTANTS PLC

■ will discuss and advise on the production of all catalogues, books and publications free of charge ■ can provide authors, editors and translators ■ has a fully equipped design and photographic studio ■ will progress projects in close consultation with the client ■ has a high turnover

of publications, so paper and print is bought very competitively ■ has a team of professionals to advise upon, produce and distribute your catalogues and books, on any subject and in any language, without you having to divert valuable staff or incur high overheads.

Call us for a **FREE** consultation.

* Museum Projects

1. BARKING & DAGENHAM
Valence House Museum

2. BARNET
Barnet Museum
Church Farmhouse Museum
London Museum of Jewish Life
Royal Air Force Museum
Stephens Collection

3. BEXLEY
Bexley Museum
David Evans Craft Centre of Silk
Erith Museum
* Crossness Engines Trust

4. BRENT
Grange Museum of Community
    History

5. BROMLEY
Bethlem Royal Hospital Archives
    and Museum
Bromley Museum
Charles Darwin Memorial
    Museum
Crystal Palace Museum

6. CAMDEN
B.O.C. Museum (The Charles King
    Collection)
British Museum
Dickens House Museum
Fenton House
Freud Museum
Great Ormond St Hospital for
    Children
Hahnemann Relics
Hampstead Museum
House of Detention
Iveagh Bequest, Kenwood
Jewish Museum
Keats House
Library and Museum of the United
    Grand Lodge of England
Museum of Zoology and
    Comparative Anatomy
Museums of the Royal College of
    Surgeons of England
Percival David Foundation of
    Chinese Art
Petrie Museum of Egyptian
    Archaeology
Pollock's Toy Museum
Royal College of Physicians
Saatchi Collection
Salvation Army International
    Heritage Centre
Sir John Soane's Museum

Thomas Coram Foundation for
    Children
Trades Union Congress Collection
University College Art Collection
University College Department of
    Geological Sciences
    Collection
Wellcome Trust Exhibitions

7. CITY OF LONDON
All Hallows By the Tower
    Undercroft Museum
Bank of England Museum
Barbican Art Gallery
BT Museum
Chartered Insurance Institute
    Museum
Clockmakers' Company Collection
Diocesan Treasury in the Crypt of
    St. Paul's Cathedral
Dr. Johnson's House
Guildhall Art Gallery
Guildhall Library (Print Room)
Museum of London
National Postal Museum
Nelson Collection, Lloyd's
Prince Henry's Room
St. Bartholomew's Hospital
    Anaesthetics Museum
St. Bartholomew's Hospital
    Archives
St. Bride's Crypt Exhibition
Tower Bridge Exhibition
* National Museum of Cartoon
    Art

8. CROYDON
Croydon Clocktower
Croydon Natural History and
    Scientific Society Museum
* Croydon Airport Society

9. EALING
Guinness Archives
Pitshanger Manor Museum
St. Bernard's Hospital Museum
Southall Railway Centre
Wilkinson Sword Museum

Museums by borough

10. ENFIELD

Forty Hall Museum
* Whitewebbs Museum of
    Transport and Industry

11. GREENWICH

Cutty Sark the Clipper Ship
Fan Museum
Greenwich Borough Museum
Museum of Artillery in the
    Rotunda
National Maritime Museum
Old Royal Observatory
Queens House
Rangers House

12. HACKNEY

Geffrye Museum
Hackney Museum
Sutton House

13. HAMMERSMITH & FULHAM

Museum of Fulham Palace
William Morris Society

14. HARINGEY

Bruce Castle Museum
Silver Studio Collection
* Markfield Beam Engine and
    Museum

15. HARROW

Cat Museum
Harrow Museum and Heritage
    Centre
Harrow School Old Speech Room
    Gallery

16. HAVERING

Upminster Tithe Barn
Upminster Windmill

17. HILLINGDON

Hillingdon Museum Service

Richard Dadd, Bethlehem Royal Hospital

18. HOUNSLOW

Boston Manor House
Chiswick House
Gillette UK Ltd
Gunnersbury Park Museum
Hogarth's House
Kew Bridge Steam Museum
Musical Museum
Osterley Park House
Syon House

19. ISLINGTON

Arsenal Football Club
Crafts Council
Islington Museum Gallery
London Canal Museum

Museum of the Honourable
    Artillery Company
Museum of the Order of St. John
Wesley's Chapel (incorporating
    Wesley's House and the
    Museum of Methodism)

20. KENSINGTON & CHELSEA

British Optical Association
    Museum
Carlyle's House
Chelsea Physic Garden
Commonwealth Institute
Kensington Palace, State
    Apartments & Royal
    Ceremonial Dress Collection
Leighton House Museum
Linley Sambourne House
London Irish Rifles

National Army Museum
Natural History Museum
Polish Institute and Sikorski
  Museum
Royal Hospital Chelsea
Science Museum
Victoria & Albert Museum

21. KINGSTON UPON THAMES
Frederick W. Paine Museum
Kingston Museum

22. LAMBETH
Black Cultural Archives/Museum
Florence Nightingale Museum
Museum of Garden History
Museum of the Moving Image
Museum of the Royal
  Pharmaceutical Society of
  Great Britain
Soseki Museum in London
Vintage Wireless Museum
* Cinema Museum
* Outsider Archive/Collection

23. LEWISHAM
Horniman Museum & Gardens

24. MERTON
Merton Heritage Centre/Museum
Wandle Industrial Museum
Wimbledon Lawn Tennis Museum
Wimbledon Society Museum
Wimbledon Windmill Museum

25. NEWHAM
East Ham Nature Reserve
North Woolwich Old Station
  Museum
* House Mill Museum Project
* Museum in Docklands
* St. Mark's Church (Silvertown
  E16)

26. REDBRIDGE
* Redbridge Museum

27. RICHMOND-UPON-THAMES
Embroiderers' Guild
Ham House
Hampton Court Palace
Kew Collections of Economic
  Botany
Kew Gardens Gallery
Kew Palace & Queen Charlotte's
  Cottage
Marble Hill House
Marianne North Gallery
Museum of Richmond
Normansfield Hospital Theatre
Orleans House Gallery
Royal Ballet School Archive
Royal Military School of Music

28. SOUTHWARK
Amalgamated Engineering and
  Electrical Union Collection
Arts Council Collection
Bankside Gallery
Bramah Tea and Coffee Museum

Wimbledon Lawn Tennis Museum

Brunel's Engine House
Clink Prison Museum
Cuming Museum
Design Museum
Dulwich Picture Gallery
Gordon Museum
Government Art Collection
H.M.S. Belfast
Imperial War Museum
Kirkaldy Testing Museum
  (Southwark)
Livesey Museum
London Fire Brigade Museum
Old Operating Theatre, Museum
  & Herb Garret
Oriental and India Office
  Collections
Pumphouse Educational Museum
Shakespeare's Globe Exhibition
South London Gallery
* Millwall F.C. Museum

29. SUTTON
Carshalton Water Tower
Heritage Centre, Honeywood
Little Holland House
Whitehall, Cheam

30. TOWER HAMLETS

Bethnal Green Museum of
    Childhood
HM Tower of London
Island History Trust
London Chest Hospital
London Gas Museum
Metropolitan Police Thames
    Division Museum
Ragged School Museum
Royal Armouries
Royal Fusiliers Museum
Royal London Hospital Museum
    and Archives Centre
Tower Hill Pageant

31. WALTHAM FOREST

Queen Elizabeth's Hunting Lodge
Vestry House Museum
William Morris Gallery

32. WANDSWORTH

Springfield Hospital Museum
Wandsworth Museum
* Puppet Centre Trust

33. WESTMINSTER

Alexander Fleming Laboratory
Alfred Dunhill Collection
Apsley House, The Wellington
    Museum
Baden-Powell House
Ben Uri Art Society
British Council Collection
British Dental Association
    Museum
Cabinet War Rooms
Courtauld Institute Galleries
Czech Memorial Scrolls Centre
Guards Museum
Inns of Court and City Yeomanry
    Museum
Institution of Mechanical
    Engineers
London Scottish Regimental
    Museum
London Toy and Model Museum
London Transport Museum

MCC Museum
Michael Faraday's Laboratory and
    Museum (Royal Institution)
Museum of Mankind
National Gallery
National Portrait Gallery
Public Record Office Museum
Queen's Gallery
Royal Academy of Arts
Royal College of Music –
    Department of Portraits &
    Performance History
Royal College of Music – Museum
    of Instruments
Royal College of Obstetricians
Royal Institute of British Architects

Bethnal Green Museum of
Childhood

Royal Opera House Archives
Tate Gallery
Theatre Museum
Twinings in the Strand
Wallace Collection
Westminster Abbey Museum
Westminster Dragoons Museum
* Benjamin Franklin House
* Girl Guides Museum
* Handel House
* Museum of Soho

AGRICULTURAL HISTORY

Bexley Museum
Upminster Tithe Barn
Upminster Windmill
Wimbledon Windmill Museum

ARCHAEOLOGY

All Hallows by the Tower
  Undercroft Museum
Barnet Museum
Bexley Museum
British Museum
Bromley Museum
Carshalton Water Tower
Croydon Natural History &
  Scientific Society
Cuming Museum

Geffrye Museum

Erith Museum
Freud Museum
Greenwich Borough Museum
Gunnersbury Park Museum
Harrow School Old Speech Room
  Gallery
Kingston Museum
Museum of London
Petrie Museum of Egyptian
  Archaeology
Pumphouse Educational Museum
St Bartholomew's Hospital
  Archives
St Bride's Crypt Museum
Sir John Soane's Museum

Tower Hill Pageant
Whitehall, Cheam
Wimbledon Society Museum

CERAMICS

Bramah Tea and Coffee Museum
British Museum
Cat Museum
Crafts Council
Croydon Clocktower (Riesco
  Gallery)
Cuming Museum
Fenton House
Leighton House Museum
Library & Museum of the United
  Grand Lodge of England
Museum of the Royal
  Pharmaceutical Society of
  Great Britain
Percival David Foundation of
  Chinese Art
Petrie Museum of Egyptian
  Archaeology
Pitshanger Manor Museum
Victoria & Albert museum
Wallace Collection
Whitehall, Cheam
William Morris Gallery

CLOCKS & WATCHES

British Museum
Clockmakers' Company Collection
Library & Museum of the United
  Grand Lodge of England
Old Royal Observatory
Victoria & Albert Museum
Wallace Collection

COMPANY HISTORY

Alfred Dunhill Collection
Bank of England Museum
BT Museum
David Evans Craft Centre of Silk
Frederick W.Paine Museum
Gillette UK Ltd
Guinness Archives
Kirkaldy Testing Museum
London Gas Museum
London Transport Museum

...ject

...um
...ffice
...ion
Twinings in the Strand
Wilkinson Sword Museum

COSTUME & TEXTILES

Barnet Museum
Bethnal Green Museum of
    Childhood
Diocesan Treasury in the Crypt of
    St Paul's Cathedral
Embroiderers' Guild
Fan Museum
Gunnersbury Park Museum
Kensington Palace, State
    Apartments & Royal
    Ceremonial Dress Collection
Museum of London
National Army Museum
Victoria & Albert Museum
Theatre Museum
Wimbledon Lawn Tennis Museum

CRAFT & DESIGN

Brooking Collection
Cat Museum
Crafts Council
Design Museum
Little Holland House
Royal Institute of British Architects
Silver Studio Collection
Victoria & Albert Museum
William Morris Gallery
William Morris Society

DECORATIVE ART

Alfred Dunhill Collection
Clockmakers' Company Collection
Courtauld Institute Galleries
Croydon Clocktower (Riesco
    Gallery)
Diocesan Treasury in the Crypt of
    St Paul's Cathedral
Fan Museum
Fenton House
Forty Hall Museum
Geffrye museum

Harrow Museum & Heritage
    Centre
Jewish Museum
Library & Museum of the United
    Grand Lodge of England
Museum of London
Nelson Collection, Lloyd's
Percival David Foundation of
    Chinese Art
Pitshanger Manor Museum
Sir John Soane's museum
Victoria & Albert museum
Wallace Collection
William Morris Gallery

FILM & PHOTOGRAPHY

Barbican Art Gallery
British Council collection
Bruce Castle Museum
Imperial War Museum
Island History Trust
Kingston Museum
London Transport Museum
Museum of London
Museum of the Moving Image
Victoria & Albert Museum
Wimbledon Society Museum

FINE ART (PAINTINGS, PRINTS, WATERCOLOURS & DRAWINGS)

Arts Council Collection
Bankside Gallery
Barbican Art Gallery
Ben Uri Art Society
Bethlem Royal Hospital Archives &
    Museum
British Council Collection
British Museum
Cat Museum
Courtauld Institute Galleries
Croydon Clocktower
Dulwich Picture Gallery
Fan Museum
Forty Hall Museum
Government Art Collection
Guildhall Art Gallery
Guildhall Library (Print Room)

Hampstead Museum
Harrow School Old Speech Room
    Gallery
Hogarth's House
Imperial War Museum
Iveagh Bequest, Kenwood
Kew Gardens Gallery
Leighton House Museum
Marble Hill House
Marianne North Gallery
Museum of London
National Army Museum
National Gallery
National Portrait Gallery
Oriental and India Office
    Collections
Orleans House Gallery
Polish Institute and Sikorski
    Museum
Queen's Gallery
Rangers House
Royal Academy of Arts
Royal College of Music,
    Department of Portraits
Royal College of Physicians
Royal Institute of British Architects
Saatchi Collection
St Bartholomew's Hospital
    Archives
Sir John Soane's Museum
South London Gallery
Syon House
Tate Gallery
Thomas Coram Foundation for
    Children
University College Art Collection
Valence Hose Museum
Victoria & Albert Museum
Wallace Collection
Wellcome Trust Exhibitions (Two
    10 Gallery)
William Morris Gallery
William Morris Society
Wimbledon Society Museum

FURNITURE

Forty Hall Museum
Geffrye Museum
Iveagh Bequest, Kenwood
Osterley Park House

Syon House
Victoria & Albert Museum
Wallace Collection

GEOLOGY

Bexley Museum
Bromley Museum
Cuming Museum
Greenwich Borough Museum
Harrow School Old Speech Room
    Gallery
Horniman Museum
Natural History Museum
University College Department of
    Geological Sciences

HISTORIC BUILDINGS

Bexley Museum
Boston Manor House
Brooking Collection
Bromley Museum
Bruce Castle Museum
Brunel's Engine House
Carlyle's House
Carshalton Water Tower
Chiswick House
Church Farmhouse Museum
Dulwich Picture Gallery
Forty Hall Museum
Gunnersbury Park museum
Ham House
Hampton Court Palace
Harrow Museum & Heritage
    Centre
Heritage Centre, Honeywood
HM Tower of London
Iveagh Bequest, Kenwood
Keats House
Kensington Palace, State
    Apartments & Royal
    Ceremonial Dress Collection
Kew Palace and Queen Charlotte's
    Cottage
Leighton House Museum
Linley Sambourne House
Little Holland house
Marble Hill House
Merton Heritage Centre
Museum of Fulham Palace

Museum of the Order of St John
Orleans House Gallery
Osterley Park House
Pitshanger Manor Museum
Prince Henry's Room
Queen Elizabeth's Hunting Lodge
Queen's House
Rangers House
St Bride's Crypt Museum
Sutton House
Syon House
Tower Bridge
Upminster Tithe Barn
Upminster Windmill
Valence House Museum
Vestry House Museum
Whitehall, Cheam
Wimbledon Windmill Museum

MEDICAL SCIENCE

Alexander Fleming Laboratory
Bethlem Royal Hospital Archives &
    Museum
British Dental Association
    Museum
British Optical Association
    Museum
British Oxygen Company Museum
    (Charles King Collection)
Chelsea Physic Garden
Florence Nightingale Museum
Freud Museum
Gordon Museum
Great Ormond St Hospital for
    Children
London Chest Hospital
Michael Faraday's Laboratory &
    Museum
Museum of the Order of St John
Museum of the Royal
    Pharmaceutical Society of
    Great Britain
Museums of the Royal College of
    Surgeons of England
National Army Museum
Old Operating Theatre, Museum
    & Herb Garret
Royal College of Obstetricians
Royal College of Physicians
Royal Hospital Chelsea

Royal London Hospital Museum &
    Archives Centre
St Bartholomew's Hospital
    Anaesthetics Museum
St Bernard's Hospital Museum
Science Museum
Springfield Hospital Museum
Veterinary Museum
Wellcome Trust Exhibitions

MILITARY HISTORY

Apsley House
Cabinet War Rooms
Guards Museum
HM Tower of London
HMS Belfast
Imperial War Museum
Inns of Court & City Yeomanry
    Museum
London Irish Rifles
London Scottish Regimental
    Museum
Museum of Artillery in the
    Rotunda
Museum of the Honourable
    Artillery Company
National Army Museum
National Maritime Museum
Polish Institute & Sikorski Museum
Royal Air Force Museum
Royal Armouries
Royal Fusiliers Museum
Royal Hospital Chelsea
Royal Military School of Music
Westminster Dragoons Museum

MULTICULTURAL

Black Cultural Archives/Museum
British Museum
Commonwealth Institute
Cuming Museum
Design Museum
Grange Museum of Community
    History
Hackney Museum
Horniman Museum
Jewish Museum
London Museum of Jewish Life
Museum of Mankind

Museums by subject

Oriental and India Office
   Collections
Polish Institute and Sikorski
   Museum
Royal Armouries
Victoria & Albert Museum

NATURAL HISTORY

Bexley Museum
Charles Darwin Memorial
   Museum
Chelsea Physic Garden
Croydon Natural History &
   Scientific Society
Cuming Museum
East Ham Nature Reserve
Greenwich Borough Museum
Harrow School Old Speech Room
   Gallery
Horniman Museum
Kew Collections of Economic
   Botany
Museum of Garden History
Museum of Zoology &
   Comparative Anatomy
Natural History Museum
Pumphouse Educational Museum

PERFORMING ARTS & SOUND ARCHIVES

British Museum
Fenton House
Horniman Museum
Museum of the Moving Image
Musical Museum
Normansfield Hospital Theatre
Puppet Centre Trust
Rangers House
Royal Ballet School Archive
Royal College of Music,
   Department of Portraits &
   Performance History
Royal College of Music, Museum
   of Instruments
Royal Military School of Music
Royal Opera House Archives
Shakespeare's Globe Exhibition
Theatre Museum
Victoria & Albert Museum
Vintage Wireless Museum

PERIOD ROOMS

Barnet Museum
Cabinet War Rooms
Carlyle's House
Carshalton Water Tower
Charles Darwin Memorial
   Museum
Church Farmhouse Museum
Courtauld Institute Galleries
Cutty Sark the Clipper Ship
Dickens House Museum
Dr Johnson's House
Erith Museum
Freud Museum
Geffrye Museum

Hackney Museum

Grange Museum of Community
   History
HMS Belfast
Imperial War Museum
Keats House
Kensington Palace, State
   Apartments & Royal
   Ceremonial Dress Collection
Leighton House Museum
Linley Sambourne House
London Fire Brigade Museum
Museum of London
Pitshanger Manor Museum

Queen Elizabeth's Hunting Lodge
Ragged School Museum
Valence House Museum
Vestry House Museum
Whitehall, Cheam
William Morris Gallery

PERSONALIA

Apsley House (Wellington)
Baden-Powell House
Brunel's Engine House
Cabinet War Rooms (Churchill)
Carlyle's House
Charles Darwin Memorial
   Museum
Dickens House Museum
Dr Johnson's House
Florence Nightingale Museum
Freud Museum
Keats House
Leighton House Museum
Linley Sambourne House
Little Holland House (Dickenson)
Michael Faraday's Laboratory &
   Museum
National Portrait Gallery
Nelson Collection, Lloyd's
Prince Henry's Room (Pepys)
Sir John Soane's Museum
Wesley's Chapel and House
William Morris Gallery
William Morris Society

POSTAL HISTORY

British Museum
Bruce Castle Museum
National Postal Museum

PUBLIC SERVICES

BT Museum
Kew Bridge Steam Museum
London Fire Brigade Museum
London Gas Museum
London Transport Museum
Metropolitan Police Thames
   Division Museum
National Postal Museum
Public Record Office Museum
 see also Medical Science

RELIGION

All Hallows by the Tower
   Undercroft Museum
British Museum
Czech Memorial Scrolls Centre
Diocesan Treasury in the Crypt of
   St Paul's Cathedral
Jewish Museum
London Museum of Jewish Life
Museum of Fulham Palace
St Bride's Crypt Exhibition
Salvation Army International
   Heritage Centre
Wesley's Chapel (incorporating
   Wesley's House and the
   Museum of Methodism)
Westminster Abbey Museum

SCIENCE & TECHNOLOGY

Alexander Fleming Laboratory
Brunel's Engine House
BT Museum
Charles Darwin Memorial
   Museum
Kew Bridge Steam Museum
Kirkaldy Testing Museum
Michael Faraday's Laboratory and
   Museum
Old Royal Observatory
Science Museum
Southall Railway Centre
Tower Bridge
Wellcome Trust Exhibitions
 see also Medical Science

SCULPTURE

Arts Council Collection
Ben Uri Art Society
British Council Collection
British Museum
Courtauld Institute Galleries
Sir John Soane's Museum
Tate Gallery
Victoria & Albert Museum
Wallace Collection

SHIPS & MARITIME HISTORY

All Hallows by the Tower
   Undercroft Museum

Cutty Sark the Clipper Ship
HMS Belfast
London Canal Museum
Museum of London
National Maritime Museum
Old Royal Observatory
Science Museum
Tower Bridge
Tower Hill Pageant

SOCIAL HISTORY

Amalgamated Engineering and
   Electrical Union Collection
Barnet Museum
Bethlem Royal Hospital Museum
   & Archives
Bexley Museum
Black Cultural Archives/Museum
Bramah Tea and Coffee Museum
Bromley Museum
Bruce Castle Museum
Chartered Insurance Institute
Church Farmhouse Museum
Clink Prison Museum
Croydon Clocktower (Lifetimes)
Crystal Palace Museum
Cuming Museum
Czech Memorial Scrolls Centre
Erith Museum
Grange Museum of Community
   History
Greenwich Borough Museum
Gunnersbury Park Museum
Hackney Museum
Hampstead Museum
Harrow Museum & Heritage
   Centre
House of Detention
Islington Museum Gallery
Island History Trust
Jewish Museum
Kew Bridge Steam Museum
Kingston Museum
Livesey Museum
London Canal Museum
London Fire Brigade Museum
London Gas Museum
London Museum of Jewish Life
Merton Heritage Centre
Museum of Fulham Palace

The Belzoni Chamber, Sir John Soane's Museum

Embroiderers' Guild
Library & Museum of the United Grand Lodge of England
MCC Museum
Museum of the Order of St John
Ragged School Museum
Salvation Army International Heritage Centre
Trades Union Congress Collection
Wimbledon Lawn Tennis Museum

SPORTING HISTORY

Arsenal Football Club Museum
Baden Powell House
Bethnal Green Museum of Childhood
British Museum
Design Museum
Hampton Court Palace
Horniman Museum
Island History Trust
MCC Museum
Museum of London
Royal Armouries
Wimbledon Lawn Tennis Museum

TOYS & GAMES

Bethnal Green Museum of Childhood
London Toy & Model Museum
Pollock's Toy Museum
Puppet Centre Trust

Museum of Garden History
Museum of London
Museum of Richmond
Public Record Office Museum
Ragged School Museum
Royal London Hospital Museum & Archives Centre
St Bride's Crypt Exhibition
Upminster Tithe Barn
Valence House Museum
Vestry House Museum
Wandle Industrial Museum
Wandsworth Museum

Wimbledon Society Museum
Wimbledon Windmill Museum

SOCIETIES & ORGANISATIONS

Amalgamated Engineering and Electrical Union Collection
Baden-Powell House
British Optical Association Foundation Collection
Chartered Insurance Institute Museum
Clockmakers' Company Collection

TRANSPORT

Gunnersbury Park Museum
Imperial War Museum
London Canal Museum
London Transport Museum
North Woolwich Old Station Museum
Science Museum
Southall Railway Centre

Exhibition and Heritage Venues

The Banqueting House
Whitehall
London SW1A 2ER
☎ 0171-930 4179

BAC
Old Town Hall
Lavender Hill
London SW11 5TF
☎ 0171-223 6557

Business Design Centre
52 Upper Street
Islington Green
London N1 0QH
☎ 0171-359 3535
Fax 0171-226 0590
(management)
Fax 0171-288 6446 (events)

Camden Arts Centre
Arkwright Road
London NW3 6DG
☎ 0171-435 2643
☎ 0171-435 5224

Contemporary Applied Arts
43 Earlham Street
London WC2H 9LD
☎ 0171-836 6993
Relocating at the end of 1995.
Please phone for new address.

Gipsy Moth IV
King William Walk
Greenwich
London SE10 9HT
☎ 0181-858 3445
Closed until summer 1996 for
restoration work.

Goethe Institute London
50 Princes Gate
Exhibition Road
London SW7 2PH
☎ 0171-411 3400

Hayward Gallery
Belvedere Road
London SE1 8XX
0171-261 0127 (recorded
information)
☎ 0171-928 3144

Institute of Contemporary Arts
Nash House
The Mall
London SW1Y 5BD
☎ 0171-930 6393 (recorded
information)
☎ 0171-930 3647 (box office)

Kathleen & May
St Mary Overy Dock
Cathedral Street
Southwark
London SE1 9DE
☎ 0171-403 3965

Lauderdale House
Waterlow Park
Highgate Hill
London N6 5HG
☎ 0181-348 8716

The Mall Galleries
The Mall
London SW1
☎ 0171-930 6844
Fax 0171-839 7830

Museum of Installation
33 Great Sutton Street
London EC1V 0DX
☎ 0171-253 0802
☎ 0171-735 7600

Old Palace, Croydon
Old Palace Road
Croydon
Surrey
☎ 0181-680 5877

Photographers' Gallery
5 Great Newport Street
London WC2H 7HY
☎ 0171-831 1772
Fax 0171-836 9704

Royal College of Art Galleries
Kensington Gore
London SW7 2EU
☎ 0171-584 5020

Serpentine Gallery
Kensington Gardens
London W2 3XA
☎ 0171-402 6075
Fax 0171-402 4103

Southside House
Wimbledon Common
London SW19 4RJ
☎ 0181-946 7643
☎ 0181-947 2491 (administrator)

Thames Barrier Visitor Centre
Unity Way
Woolwich
London SE18 5NJ
☎ 0181-854 1373

Whitechapel Art Gallery
80-82 Whitechapel High Street
London E1 7QX
☎ 0171-522 7888
Fax 0171-377 1685

Archives & Libraries

Ashmole Archive
Department of Classics
King's College London
Strand
London WC2R 2LS
☎ 0171-836 5454 ext 1093

Book Trust
Book House
45 East Hill
London SW18 2QZ
☎ 0181-870 9055

British Library
Humanities & Social Sciences
Great Russell Street
London WC1B 3DG
☎ 0171-636 1544

Useful addresses

British Olympic Library
1 Wandsworth Plain
London SW18 1EH
☎ 0181-871 2677

Fawcett Library
London Guildhall University
Old Castle Street
London E1 7NT
☎ 0171-320 1189

Hammersmith & Fulham Archives
& Local History Centre
The Lilla Huset
191 Talgarth Road
London W6 8BJ
☎ 0181-741 5159
☎ 0181-748 3020 ext 3850
Please telephone to make an
appointment

Kennel Club Library
Kennel Club
1-5 Clarges Street
Piccadilly
London W1Y 8AB
☎ 0171-499 0844
Fax 0171-495 6162

Lambeth Palace Library
Lambeth Palace Road
London SE1 7JU
☎ 0171-928 6222

Lewisham Local Studies Centre
Lewisham Library
199-201 Lewisham High Street
London SE13 6LG
☎ 0181-297 0682

Marx Memorial Library
37a Clerkenwell Green
London EC1R 0DU
☎ 0171-253 1485

National Film & Television Archive
21 Stephen Street
London W1P 2LN
☎ 0171-255 1444
☎ 0171-957 8969
Fax 0171-580 7503

National Monuments Record
Kemble Drive
Swindon SN2 2GZ
☎ 01793-414 600

National Sound Archive
(British Library)
29 Exhibition Road
London SW7 2AS
☎ 0171-412 7430
Fax 0171-412 7416

NSPCC Archive
42 Curtain Road
London EC2A 3NH
☎ 0171-825 2500

Sainsbury's Archives
J Sainsbury plc
Stamford House
Stamford Street
London SE1 9LL
☎ 0171-921 6510

Science Museum Library
Imperial College Road
London SW7 5NH
☎ 0171-938 8234
☎ 0171-938 8213

CITY LIVERY COMPANIES

Apothecaries Hall
Blackfriars Lane
London EC4V 6EJ
☎ 0171-236 1189

Armourers & Brasiers Hall
81 Coleman Street
London EC2R 5BJ
☎ 0171-606 1199

Clothworkers Hall
Dunster Court
Mincing Lane
London EC3R 7AH
☎ 0171-623 7041

Drapers Hall
Throgmorton Avenue
London EC2N 2DQ
☎ 0171-588 5001

Fishmongers Hall
London Bridge
London EC4R 9EL
☎ 0171-626 3531

Goldsmiths Hall
Foster Lane
London EC2V 6BN
☎ 0171-606 7010

Haberdashers Hall
Staining Lane
London EC2V 4TE
☎ 0171-606 0967

Ironmongers Hall
Shaftsbury Place
London EC2Y 8AA
☎ 0171-606 2725

Mercers Hall
Ironmonger Lane
London EC2V 8HE
☎ 0171-726 4991

Merchant Taylors Hall
30 Threadneedle Street
London EC2Y 8AY
☎ 0171-588 7606

Painter-Stainers Hall
9 Little Trinity Lane
London EC4V 2AD
☎ 0171-236 6258

Pewterers Hall
Oat Lane
London EC2V 7DE
☎ 0171-606 9363

RELATED & PROFESSIONAL BODIES

Age Exchange Reminiscence
Centre
11 Blackheath Village
London SE3 9LA
☎ 0181-318 9105
Fax 0181-318 0060

Association of In dependent
Museums
c/o Andrew Patt erson
Hotties Science a nd Arts Centre
PO Box 68
Chalon Way
St Helens
Merseyside WA9   1LL
☎ 01744-22766

Architectural Ass ociation School
of Architecture
34-36 Bedford Square
London WC1B 3 ES
☎ 0171-636 0974

Association for B usiness
Sponsorship of the Arts
Nutmeg House
60 Gainsford Street
Butler's Wharf
London SE1 2NY
☎ 0171-378 8143
Fax 0171-407 7527

British Associatio n of Friends of
Museums
31 Southwell Park Road
Camberley
Surrey GU15 3Q G
☎ 01276-66617

British Council
10 Spring Garde ns
London SW1A 2 BN
☎ 0171-930 8466

British Tourist Au thority
Head Office
Thames Tower
Black's Road
London W6 9EL
☎ 0181-846 90O0

Contemporary A rt Society
20 John Islip Str e et
London SW1P 4 LL
☎ 0171-821 53 23

Wellcome Trust Exhibitions

Council for British Archaeology
Bowes Morrel House
111 Walmgate
York YO1 2UA
☎ 01904-671 417

Department of National Heritage
2-4 Cockspur Street
London SW1Y 5BQ
☎ 0171-211 6000

English Heritage
(Historic Buildings & Monuments
Commission)

Fortress House
Savile Row
London W1X 1AB
☎ 0171-973 3000

English Tourist Board
Thames Tower
Black's Road
London W6 9EL
☎ 0181-846 9000

Ephemera Society
84 Marylebone High Street
London W1M 3DE
☎ 0171-935 7305
☎ 0171-487 4669

79

Useful addresses

International Council of Museums
(ICOM)
Maison de l'UNESCO
1 rue Miollis
F-75732 Paris
Cedex 15
France
☎ 47-34-05-00
Fax 47-06-78-62

Library Association
7 Ridgmount Street
London WC1E 7AE
☎ 0171-636 7543

London Arts Board
Elme House
133 Long Acre
Covent Garden
London WC2E 9AF
☎ 0171-240 1313

London Boroughs Grants Unit
5th Floor, Regal House
London Road
Twickenham TW1 3QS
☎ 0181-891 5021

London MAGDA
(Museums and Galleries Disability
Association)
c/o Rebecca McGinnis
Education Department
Victoria & Albert Museum
Cromwell Road
London SW7 2RL
☎ 0171-938 8632
Fax 0171-938 86351

London Tourist Board and
Convention Bureau
26 Grosvenor Gardens
Victoria
London SW1W 0DU
☎ 0171-730 3450
(administration)
☎ 0171-730 3488 (tourist
information)

London Voluntary Service Council
356 Holloway Road
London N7 6PA
☎ 0171-700 8107

Museums and Galleries Disability
Association
(MAGDA)
c/o The Secretary
Kathy Niblett
City Museum and Art Gallery
Stoke-on-Trent ST1 3DW
☎ 01782-202 173

Museums Association
42 Clerkenwell Close
London EC1R 0PA
☎ 0171-608 2933

Museum Documentation
Association
Lincoln House
347 Cherry Hinton Road
Cambridge CB1 4DH
☎ 01223-242 848

Museums & Galleries Commission
16 Queen Anne's Gate
London SW1H 9AA
☎ 0171-233 4200

Museum Training Institute
1st Floor, Glyde House
Glyde Gate
Bradford BD5 0UP
☎ 01274-391 056
☎ 01274-391 092

National Art Collections Fund
Millais House
7 Cromwell Place
London SW7 2JN
☎ 0171-225 4800
Fax 0171-225 4848

National Campaign for the Arts
Francis House
Francis Steet
London SW1P 1DE
☎ 0171-828 4448
Fax 0171-931 9959

South Eastern Museums Service
Ferroners House
Barbican
London EC2Y 8AA
☎ 0171-600 0219
Fax 0171-600 2581